"We come to love not by finding a perfect person, but by learning to see an imperfect person perfectly"

Sam Keen

The Joy of Marriage

Why some marriages work and others fail

Andrew C. Phiri
With Norah Phiri

Printed in the USA for worldwide distribution

ISBN-13: 978-9982998611
ISBN-10: 9982998617

Unless otherwise indicated all scripture quotations were taken from the Holy Bible - King James Version © Cambridge University Press.

Note on citations: A name followed by date in parenthesis indicates the source of the referenced text. Find a matching entry in *References* for full details of the item.

Disclaimer: While the publisher has taken great care to ensure accuracy of facts in the preparation of this material, it reserves the right to revise this publication and make changes to its content from time to time without notice, and hence will not accept any legal responsibility or liability for any errors or omissions from the book or the consequences thereof. Furthermore take note that products and services mentioned in this book may be trademarks of their respective owners; the publisher and author makes no claim to these trademarks.

This book is available on Amazon and other e-stores.

MiTe Publishing Ltd ● PO Box 37919 ● Lusaka ● Zambia

Acknowledgements

Special thanks to:

Jesse M. Nzima for proofreading the manuscripts.

Hubert D'Souza for designing the book cover.

Norah Phiri for saying *"I do"* when **Rev. James Veremu** asked her at the altar if she would accept me as her husband. Being a perfect companion and love of my life, she has made this book possible. Together we are still exploring and learning the intriguing world of love!

For permission to reproduce images and jokes, the authors and publisher wish to thank the following:

Cartoon-Impact.com, cartoons on pages 23,115, and 134.

Justin Ezzi, joke on page 137.

Suresh Sawant, cartoon on page 101.

For bearing us for nine months, and enduring the challenges that comes with raising a child as a mother, Norah and I salute:

Agness Phiri and **Gertrude Daka**.

Effort has been made to contact copyright holders before publication of this material. Even so, in some cases it was not possible. If contacted, MiTe Publishing Ltd will ensure that full credit is given at the earliest opportunity.

To
Christian couples, those about to marry, and
anyone of marriageable age.

CONTENTS

Questions & Answers

Some questions have been asked through email correspondence and others during counselling sessions. Find answers on the page numbers indicated against each question below.

Question   **Page**

Q1. *"I love my wife but I get attracted to*   157
a certain beautiful woman at my
work place. What is making matters
worse is that she also seems to be
interested in me because I have
observed her intimate advances
towards me. I have to be frank that I
am really getting attracted to her.
Her looks are so appealing. I have
prayed for God to deliver me out of
this sin but each time I happen to
start chatting with her, it suddenly
seems so innocent for me to love her.
What can I do?"

Q2. *"We have been taught that it is a sin*   160
to   practise   family   planning,
especially using methods of condoms
or contraceptive pills. So, with my
wife we've tried to use the natural
method but which is not working
well for us. We now have three
children and are expecting our

fourth. We sometimes get tempted to start using condoms but then we read Genesis 38:8-9 and are reminded that children come from God and it is sinful to waste them in a condom."

Q3. *"My husband and I are both in employment but yet are always broke. This situation many times makes us to argue and quarrel. His uncles, nephews, grandparents, and siblings are always asking for money and he doesn't seem to know the words, 'Sorry, I am not able to help this time'. He will give them money even when we are in need of it at home. I know we ought to help our families but should it be done at the expense of our family's joy?"* 165

Q4. *"My wife seems to be never interested in sex. We only have it a few times and she doesn't seem to fully participate in those moments. I feel starved. What can I do for her to be in love with me?"* 168

Q5. *"My husband always chats with a female friend on the phone. He is ever on WhatsApp talking to her. When I confront him about it, he* 172 *always explains that it is a business partner he is talking to. My worry is that he is ever so protective of his phone. He cannot leave it behind or allow me to touch or make a call using his phone. When I request for his phone to make a call, he would rather give me money to buy airtime and use my phone. My worries once heightened, when I once overhead him say (in a low-tone voice), 'I miss you' to someone I suspected to be the lady he is flirting with. How do I handle this situation seeing that I can't approach him over a matter I don't have concrete evidence?"*

Q6. *"My relatives do not get along with my wife. They say that since she came into my life I have stopped being supportive of the family. And I have noticed that whenever my mother and siblings visit our home, my wife always gets moody because of mom who always wants to advise her on various things - how to manage a home, how to cook, etc. I feel my wife gets intimidated at this but she has a problem of not opening up to me. What can I do?"* 176

Preface

"Houses and wealth are inherited from parents", wrote King Solomon, *"but a prudent wife is from the LORD"* (Proverbs 19:14). These words are not a reality in the lives of many married couples. Many husbands cannot speak of their wives as being a gift from the Lord. Likewise many wives are enduring their husbands, instead of enjoying their company. However, it is encouraging to know that there are also some couples who have lived through old age enjoying their marriages. I have come to know and befriend a few of such elderly couples and have learnt a lot from them. Good marriages leave footprints on the sands of time which should be followed by those who are humble enough and willing to learn. Unfortunately, many young men and women have misled themselves into problems through wrong advice, often obtained from their

fellow young peers. The results should be obvious: young couples keep breaking up whilst the old folk are till as intact as a brick to cement. Whilst most elderly folk have nothing much to show in terms of a new car, an iPad, or expensive outfit, modern young couples are enthused into these things as a measure of their joy and success. If a young couple would apply their heart to learn, they would discover that the glue of virtue is what has held elderly couples together in experiencing the joy of marriage.

A couple should invest time in learning about what makes some marriages fail and others succeed. It is interesting to note that many people invest over 25 years of their lives educating themselves into careers that will take them into contracts with institutions of formal employment. Much neglected is the fact that there is a greater institution which affects many aspects of one's life, and this not for a limited period of a contract but a lifetime, until the day one bids farewell to this world. This institution is marriage. Very few invest time to educate themselves into it. This probably explains why marriage is the one institution with the highest number of failures. And, is it not true that no matter how successful a person can be in his or her financial and other areas of life, if their marriage is in ruins, their life, ultimately, is a failure. If you are in such a situation, don't despair. There is hope if you are humble enough and willing to learn.

THE JOY OF MARRIAGE is a collection of lessons I have taught at the bi-monthly *Believers'*

Couples Fellowship meetings held in Lusaka, Zambia. Due to the many questions people ask during the meetings, counselling sessions, and through email, I have come to realise that whilst much concentration in many churches is on mysteries of the Bible, the marriage and family life of many believers is slowly deteriorating in the background. One reason for this unfortunate situation has been the lack of sufficient attention being given to the subject.

Many husbands and wives portray adorable images of peace and love on *Facebook*, *Whatsapp* and *Twitter* picture profiles, but yet are going through a depressing life, devoid of true love and fellowship with their spouses. Some couples have taken to prayer and fasting to cast out "demons of confusion" out of their marriages and others have fallen by the deception of "prophets" who would claim to "see" what went wrong in their lives. Nine times out of ten such efforts have never yielded results. What is more, many marriages in such situations often deteriorate further into separation and divorce. Didn't God hear the prayers? Was He unjust? Did He overlook the sincere prayer of a suffering spouse? Did He let evil spirits ruin the marriage of a believer? Not so.

The *JOY OF MARRIAGE* dispels the myth of always blaming marriage and family problems on demons. Far from being mystic most problems in marriage are due to the lack of knowledge. Yes, ignorance has robbed many marriages of their joy. As in the words of the prophecy of Hosea, "*My people are destroyed for lack of knowledge*"

(Hosea 4:6). The most powerful gift God endowed mankind with is free will. Our present lives are a sum total of what we know and what have been choosing *to do* in the past and in the present. Right now you are reading these words because you want to know something.

In this book I share information about how poor financial management, a poor sex-life, and a large family beyond one's capacity can lead to many problems in marriage. Whilst many counsellors try to solve a problem presented to them by trimming off its 'leaves', in this book we endeavour to deal with the 'root' cause of many problems in marriage by looking at the big picture which will reveal a nexus of factors that affects the success of a marriage.

There are certain things in this book that are specifically essential for men and other things which are more important for women. However, it will be good for a couple to read and study the book together. I requested Norah, my wife, for her notes on insights she usually shares to women who are about to get married and those who are already married but are going through marital problems. It is our hope and prayer that you will find this book useful.

In Christ,

Andrew C. Phiri
Lusaka, Zambia.

Introduction

What is Marriage?

"Therefore shall a man leave his father and his mother, and shall cleave unto his wife: and they shall be one flesh" (Genesis 2:24) – these are words which came by inspiration through the lips of the first husband on earth. These words tell us what happens when a man and woman marry, they:

1. Leave their parents
2. Cleave to each other, and
3. Become one flesh

LEAVING PARENTS is not just about moving from your parents' house to go and establish your own. It also involves stopping to depend on your parents' financial support. Likewise, it also means your parents ending their dependence on you if they had been doing so. Of course, certain situations could be understandable or exceptional but it often happens in some societies that no sooner does a new couple get married than siblings and parents begin to exert pressure of incessant financial requests on them. With time the young couple begin to get so stressed up. Later when children appear in the home, the couple are too financially constrained to enrol them in good schools, provide proper medical cover, or arrange for vacations with them.

It so happens in such situations that a relative who asks for money from such a couple may not realise that many others have also asked for the same. In some situations, relatives begin to dislike and even gossip about the wife and also continuously label her as a hindrance to the regular help they once used to receive from their relative. In Africa, and I believe many other Third World regions of the world, this has become normal and many people view it as a noble responsibility that new couples ought to proudly embrace. Well, I call it a *cultural fallacy*! Believe it or not, this attitude of people living as though someone owes them something (failing to own up responsibility for their lives) has contributed greatly to African societies' poverty. Unfortunately the fallacy is so hardwired into people's minds that many see it as a virtue. To talk or teach against the fallacy would almost be regarded as a taboo. I could see this attitude among believers in the church I pastor. One day I decided to drop the 'bomb' as I taught at the Believers Couples Fellowship meeting. I said to the couples:

You should help your relatives as much as your resources can allow and not to the extent of depriving your wife and innocent children; and remember to raise your children in a way that will make them responsible adults who will not pass on the fallacy to their generation. Above all, do what you can now to secure a stable financial future so that when you get old you won't become a burden to your children; never produce children in order to use them as insurance for your old age. The Scripture teaches that, "Children ought not to lay up for the parents, but the parents for the children" (2 Corinthians 12:14). Teach these to your children when they mature and tell them to pass it on to their children as well. If this cycle continues and the Lord tarries, Africa may become a better responsible society. Is it not interesting to note that in many developed countries children begin their lives on a rich-level of where their parents left off. Children have an inheritance to get started on which they will in turn leave to their children. In a couple of generations to come the future of other children is already well-secured. In Africa, on the other hand, children inherit problems left by their parents; a young man who should concentrate on building his life finds himself tied with so much responsibility of taking care of relatives, including his siblings whom his parents could not afford to take care of.

When two people get married they become an independent self-sustaining unit. It is for this reason that a man needs to know what he is doing when he decides to propose to a woman; he will become a head, shelter, and provider for the woman and children that will come into the family. A married man who is ever dependent on his parents for guidance or on what decisions to make, is no different from a chair with shaky legs, failing to provide the needed support for someone who sits on it as it can at any time fall thus risking the safety of the one seated on it. And indeed, there are many womenfolk who are deeply hurting inside because their husbands can't exercise their authority as men; the men are 'headless husbands'. This is one thing a woman has to seriously consider before she says "*I do*" to a man.

Before you say "*I do*"

Modern young ladies have no idea about what qualities to see in a man before they agree to his proposal. What is more, it is now becoming common for youngsters to start love relationships through social media, a very limited platform to give you information about the personality of your spouse-to-be. Many young people are so obsessed with the fictitious Hollywood models of smart and neat outlooks and exaggerated accents. Sadly, the fiction movie ends on the day they get married; reality sets in and it is then they realise the trouble they have got themselves into.

Here are three important questions to ask before accepting a man's proposal:

1. Is he a man who knows who he is and what he is looking for in life or is merely a *"reed shaken with the wind"*[1] staggering at each blowing piece of advice or opinion? Remember this is the man you will be relying on as your *"head."* A good man is not only focussed and consistent in life but has a firm faith which is grounded in the Word of God. Many women trapped themselves into perpetual trouble after getting married to an unbeliever. God's Word admonishes us to marry someone who is *"in the Lord"* (1 Corinthians 7:39).

2. Does he look wise-enough to govern the affairs of his own house without being dependent on what his brothers, sisters, or parents have to say? There are homes in which a man or a woman is remotely controlled by demands or comments of parents, siblings, or other relatives. Such homes are houses built on sand, not rock; one day a stronger wind will blow and the marriage will disintegrate.[2]

3. Is he a man who will treasure and respect you as his queen; protecting you from the

---

[1] Ephesians 5:23
[2] Matthew 7:24-27

slanders and gossips of other people? A good husband will never disrespect, demean or question his wife's integrity in the presence of relatives, friends, or anyone else. He will make her respectable and people will treat her as such.

"Sorry—I'm used to meeting on Skype"

CLEAVING TO EACH OTHER is not a one day occurrence; it is a process. In fact the English word "*Marriage*" in Greek comes from the word "*gameo*", explains Dr Munroe; and this word is derived from the same root as the English word "*gem*". You are probably familiar with *gem* as it refers to precious things like diamonds. The interesting thing about the word *gem* is that it means to "*fuse together*":

Precious gems such as diamonds, rubies,

emeralds, and sapphires are formed far underground out of ordinary elements that are subjected to great heat and massive pressure over an extended period of time. Heat, pressure, and time working together can transform even the most common material into something extraordinary...Coal is formed when partially decomposed wood or other plant matter is combined with moisture in an airless environment under intense heat and pressure...Coal that remains in the earth long enough – thousands of years longer – under continuous heat and pressure eventually is transformed into diamond (Munroe, 2002, p.19).

A lot is involved in the process of fusing together. The trouble is many men go into marriage to enjoy the *pleasure* of sex but not the *pressure* of the fusing of the two lives. Unfortunately, what they find in marriage is a personality different from what they saw during courting. Pleasures of cone-ice creams may cease as pressures of monthly budgets begin. Tones change, from "*Hi Sweety*" to "*Hhaa, Norah!*" What makes the process of fusing challenging is that it involves the coming together of different behaviors, priorities, and histories. Again Myles explains it well:

Marriage is never just the coming together of two people, but a collision of their histories. It is a clash of cultures, experiences, memories, and habits. Marriage is the beautiful accommodation of another lifetime...When you marry someone, you marry more than just a person; you "marry"...a complete history of experiences...Adjusting to these differences is critical to marital survival. Unfortunately, many marriages fail on precisely this point. (Munroe, 2002, p.20).

BECOMING ONE FLESH: This is an important element of the process of cleaving together in marriage; it occurs when a couple consummate their love in sexual union. This union leads to the formation of a new human being on earth. And although the climax of the sexual pleasure only occurs for a few seconds, the child that is conceived from the process will last for a lifetime. That child enters this world ignorant of so many things. Through time he or she will begin to have a character which will be shaped by various influences that surround him or her. It is the duty of the parents to ensure that their child grows up into a responsible adult with a sense of purpose and faith in God. This is not an easy task to do on one or two children in a busy world which requires so much of your time at work, and attending to so many other demands. However being busy should never be an excuse for neglecting to mentor a life that you brought into the world; that child never wrote a letter of application to be born; it is your sole responsibility to nourish, fend and inspire it to grow to its full aspirations. But, big trouble for Africans here again: people produce children in numbers way beyond their capacity to manage them. Genesis 1:27 is the scripture often cited for this carelessness. One wonders whether the task was given to one couple. And even if that were the case (for a couple to multiply and fill up the earth), isn't the task almost already accomplished as the United Nations organisation is now even worried about the rising global population?

What we see in all this is that marriage is the process of a man and woman *fusing* into one. Knowledge about what this process entails, as was briefly explained in the foregoing, is crucial for experiencing the joy of marriage. On the converse, ignorance is what has led to the destruction of many marriages. So, knowledge or information is what determines whether a marriage will succeed or not. In this book I hope to go some distance in sharing information that I hope and trust may inspire you to experience the joy of marriage.

IN EDEN MARRIAGE BEGAN when a man awoke and found his woman. This new creature, although being also a human being, was different in form and emotional make-up but yet so complementary to the male. This design had a purpose. Adam knew that purpose immediately he opened his eyes and beheld the beautiful figure of a woman standing before him. He had a revelation of what this beautiful figure standing before him was meant for; it was for him to unite with her in love and become one flesh. From this we can deduce that it is a man's responsibility to understand the complementary difference which exists between him and his wife. The failure to understand this difference and its purpose is the beginning of the failure of marriage. It is important to know that a woman was a figure so designed for the man. But designed for what? Just for the man to have sex with her?

1.
A Woman – God's gift to man

"When God gave a man a wife, He gave him the best thing He could give him, outside of salvation"

William Branham

"Let her be as the loving hind and pleasant roe; let her breasts satisfy thee at all times; and be thou ravished always with her love"

Proverbs 5:19

God's gift to man

"When God gave a man a wife, He gave him the best thing He could give him, outside of salvation" said Rev. William Branham[3]. *"Houses and wealth are inherited from parents"*, wrote King Solomon, *"but a prudent wife is from the LORD"* (Proverbs 19:14, NIV).

These words are true. However, we live in a world of so much immorality and filth until some believers avoid talk about the important topics of love and intimacy. Some even seem to get so 'spiritual' until they treat the three-letter word *s-e-x* as though it was invented by the devil. What is more, the indecent women who love to dress immorally by exposing their bodies have made it look like the attractive breasts, legs and hips of a woman are evil in themselves. But, not so. The Bible has some places where love-words are used which in modern language would be described as sexually graphic. Consider the following passages of Scripture for example:

Sustain me with raisins, refresh me with apples, for I am sick with love. I can feel his left hand under my head and his right hand embraces me (Song of Solomon 2:5-6, Amplified Bible).

Let her be as the loving hind and pleasant roe; let her breasts satisfy thee at all times; and be

---

[3] Branham, 1965.p.10.

thou ravished always with her love (Proverbs 5:19).

How beautiful are thy feet with shoes, O prince's daughter! the joints of thy thighs are like jewels, the work of the hands of a cunning workman. Thy navel is like a round goblet, which wanteth not liquor: thy belly is like an heap of wheat set about with lilies. Thy two breasts are like two young roes that are twins (Song of Solomon 7:1).

Yes, the beautiful legs, thighs and breasts of a woman are *"the work of the hands of a cunning workman"* and that *"workman"* is God! The trouble is, people have wondered away from their maker and now abuse their bodies into fornication and adultery.

Someone once said that a wedding ring is the smallest handcuff ever made and so a person ought to choose their prison mate carefully. But that's not true; a wedding ring is a beautiful tag of freedom – the freedom to love and embrace your spouse without having any guilt feelings of fornication.

The attraction of love between the male and female was made to be enjoyed within the confines of marriage. A woman ought to dress decently by covering her body in public. Her nudity is just for the eyes of her beloved husband. But like anything made which is not used according to the manufacturer's prescription will be abused, so mankind has abused his body and sex life. The abuse has resulted into hurt, hate and various diseases. Even so, a believer in God should know that marriage was made by God for mankind and should bring the satisfaction of joy and peace. But in many marriages today, husbands and wives are bonded together out of enduring each other, not love. This is not good. However, if you are in such a condition please be informed that the present situation of your marriage still has a chance to turn around into a joyful experience. It can happen to you if you are humble enough to learn, and also sincere enough to admit mistakes which will be brought to your attention in these lessons.

The headship of a man

An important concept to understand in marriage is that a man is the head over a wife (Eph.5:23). Now, this headship is not all about making decisions in the house. It also means that, if a marriage or family begins to fail, no matter what justifications a man can give of how wrong his wife is, the blame will ultimately land on his shoulders. A man ought to take responsibility of his family by demonstrating wise leadership. Remember what happened in the Garden of Eden when the woman sinned? Did God call out to Eve? No. God called out to Adam:

"Where art thou?"

Let us ask ourselves this question in another way – Where am I; am I still at the place where:

- *I still love my wife the way I used to when I just married her?*

- *I am kind and gracious to her?*

- *I still take her out, away from the noise of the city, into a place where we are alone to talk about our life, plans and love for each other?*

- *I relate with her as a "weaker vessel"[4], who needs my patience and empathy about the many things that can stress her emotionally?*

- *Do I ever appreciate her for her hard work around the house, or have I been selfish and consumed in only what concerns me?*

- *When is the last time I bought her a beautiful outfit, and yes, a panty or a bra?*

It so happens in many marriages that when a man has just married his wife, the care and feelings of love for her seem to be at their height, so to speak. At this point care seems to naturally flow from his heart. But with time, there is a falling away from *"the first love"*; with time, instead of a couple enjoying each other's company, they begin to

---

[4] 1 Peter 3:7

endure each other. Husbands, may we be admonished to never let the honeymoon experience with our wives die. William Branham on this issue:

> *Talking about men losing their affections for their wives and not loving them as they did when they were sweethearts, Shame on you! You ought to do it; she's your sweetheart...that's the part she should be and you should treat her like that. Oh, never let that little honeymoon cease* (Branham, 1957).

Sadly, many ignore the danger sign of diminishing affection for their spouse, taking it to be a normal thing that happens to everyone. What a man may not realise is that the lack of affection being given to his wife will slowly start eating up her joy. This situation will be worsened when she begins to share her agonies with people who are going through the same unpleasant experience.

Getting advice from wrong sources

When I was getting married many married folk would tell me that marriage is a tough club which one has to endure; "*love doesn't last very long in marriage*", many would emphasise. Well, knowing that a person ultimately becomes what he allows his mind to feed on, I was careful in listening and evaluating such advice. Notice also that what the mind constantly hears it gradually believes. The danger is, one can never live beyond his beliefs. It is for this reason that you ought to "*take heed to what you hear*" (Mar. 4:24).

What some people may advise you is based on their failures which may have resulted from something they could have in the past lacked in character and in turn think it is something which applies to everyone. You ought to learn how to distinguish facts from speculation and speculation from exaggeration. In my early years of marriage I decided to look around for people whose marriages stood the test of time but yet were still joyous and lovely. Fortunately, I have been in the company of such couples; a number of them are old but are still as loving as though it is when they are courting with their wives.[5] Such are couples one needs to look up to as role models. Unfortunately many modern young couples only feed on peers' advice which many times is ungodly and misleading. And just as a blind who is led by another blind person end up in a ditch so are such modern marriages.

Knowledge about principles that govern a successful marriage should be sought from couples with a testimony of success. If someone has overcome in his or her marriage life, the victory is a footprint on the sands of time to let others know that they can also be victorious. Life is a choice. You

---

[5] At *Believers' Assembly* church, we hold couples meetings about once every two months where various topics about marriage are taught. Once in a while an elderly couple (whose marriage has been a good success) is invited to share the values which helped them enjoy their relationship. If you desire to attend some of these meetings you can email us and we will be glad to give you a schedule of forthcoming meetings (Email: *voiceoftheword@live.com*).

have to decide what you want to believe and what to make out of your marriage. But before we go much further, let us ask ourselves this question:

What really makes some marriages fail and others to succeed?

A common fallacy some people believe is that some couples are successful because they are gifted in character. But the truth is that character is not a gift but a victory. In the Bible we are told in several places about the rewards which will be given to overcomers. So, if a Christian life is about overcoming, it goes without saying that the same can be extended to marital problems; they ought to be overcome. But, what problems? Well, we can only identify problems if we know how an ideal situation ought to look like. So, we should begin with the question, *what makes a marriage successful?*

A successful marriage is one built on the good foundation of excellent:

- Communication
- Sound financial management, and
- Enjoyable sex-life.

Do not underrate any of these three things; they interlock, and a loss of quality in, or attention to, any of them can result into undesirable consequences. It is important that a pastor of a church conducts routine meetings (say once every two months) where these matters are taught to couples. Unfortunately, in many churches, much focus has been on mysteries of the Bible and yet the marriage and family life of many couples are dying slowly, causing moods, tensions and sadness in homes. Most believers are so enthused about *faith* and the *hope* of the rapture, but yet neglect *love*, a thing that presently and continuously robes them of their joy. It is important to know that a bad marriage and unhealthy family atmosphere ultimately affects your joy in the Lord.

Contrary to what most ministers think, the strength of a church's membership is not measured in terms of how many people it has, but how many family units it consists of. And, if most families are unhappy and unspiritual, this condition will ultimately manifest in the church at large.

A pastor should have, among his top priorities, regular programmes that educate couples about how to build sound and happy families. One important principle to emphasise in such meetings is the crucial role of communication in marriage.[6]

---

[6] For a pastor to effectively teach and inspire couples and their families in church he ought to lead by example. It is for this reason that the Scripture admonishes that *"A bishop then must be blameless, the husband of one wife, vigilant, sober, of good behaviour, given to hospitality, apt to teach... One that ruleth well his own house, having his children in subjection with all gravity; (For if a man know not how to rule his own house, how shall he take care of the church of God?)"* (1 Timothy 3:2-5).

Have some laughter

A woman awoke during the night and did not find her husband in bed. She put on her robe and went downstairs. He was sitting at the kitchen table with a cup of coffee in front of him. He appeared to be in deep thought, just staring at the wall. She saw him wipe a tear from his eye and take a sip of his coffee.

"What's the matter dear? Why are you down here at this time of night?" she asked.

"Do you remember twenty years ago when we were dating and you were only 16?" he asked.

"Yes, I do" she replied.
"Do you remember when your father caught us making love?"
"Yes, I remember."
"Do you remember when he shoved that shotgun in my face and said, 'Either you marry my daughter or spend twenty years in jail?"

"Yes, I do" she said.

He wiped another tear from his cheek and said, "*You know...I would have gotten out today*."

2.
Communication

"The Christian attitude does not mean that there is anything wrong about sexual pleasure, any more than about the pleasure of eating. It means that you must not isolate that pleasure and try to get it by itself, any more than you ought to try to get the pleasures of taste without swallowing and digesting, by chewing things and spitting them out again"

C.S. Lewis

"I sleep, but my heart waketh: it is the voice of my beloved that knocketh, saying, Open to me, my sister, my love, my dove, my undefiled: for my head is filled with dew, and my locks with the drops of the night"

Song of Solomon 5:2

It is *lust* not *love*!

I once had a tense counselling session; the woman, sitting beside her husband, could not hold back her tears as she countered the accusation of the husband about denying him sex. She sobbed as she explained:

> *My husband only gets in bed to satisfy himself; I rarely reach orgasm. It seems he is only interested in my body and not me. He only treats me kindly and lovingly when he is thirsty for sex. After sex, he is no longer loving and caring.*

This is a common problem among couples: a husband being in a happy and kind mood only on the nights he desires sex with his wife. This is a woman whose hands he has stopped holding as lovingly as he used to when he was courting her; and his voice tone towards her is constantly cold and unfriendly.[7] The day he suddenly gets in a happy mood now becomes an indication to his wife that he is thirsty for sex. Such behaviour is unbecoming for a Christian husband! It is not only wrong but hypocritical and wicked. Such a man is bribing a wife with a temporal fake appeasement just in order to quench his lustful feelings. It is lust, not love, that he has for his wife. Such a sexual

---

[7] Surprisingly, some men when speaking to other women at their workplaces or elsewhere show more kindness and tenderness to them than their wives at home.

relationship will at many times only see a man reaching the height of excitement (satisfaction) in a sexual encounter while leaving the woman more dissatisfied (and even hurt) in her heart. Furthermore, this situation of a woman always not getting satisfied in sex leads to some other uglier problems (listed below).

Some common symptoms of an unsatisfied wife.

The following are usually common symptoms of an unsatisfied woman:

- *Moods*

The woman always feeling low and unhappy. It is important to know that the sexual experience has various stages for a woman, different from a man; from the initial arousal through to the extreme point of pleasure known as the *orgasm*. If a woman is always 'turned on' but is never let to reach the orgasm, this can result into the discomfort from the unsatisfied sexual arousals. This upset can cause her to develop ill feelings towards her uncaring husband. She will begin to see him as a man who only uses her as a sex object, without true love and affection for her. It is interesting to note that there are many husbands who complain about their wives being moody but yet being very ignorant of the fact that they are the causers of the unfortunate situation. This is not a small problem; a good number of marriages have broken up owing to this problem. In some uglier situations the problem would exacerbate to a point where an unsatisfied spouse commits fornication or adultery to relieve the sexual desire. Even so, such an occurrence always turns out to be the last nail one would have put in his or her own coffin.

- *No interest in sex*

A wife who is starved of orgasm may gradually lose interest in sex. She will see sex as a useless and cumbersome exercise. This is not normal. A woman in a healthy marriage would often enjoy the joy of meeting and embracing with her husband. So, the state of despising this intimacy could many times be an indication of a marital problem. Again, instead of the man complaining about the problem, it would be wise for him to be honest and sincere with himself while carrying out an introspection of how he has been handling the sexual aspect of his marriage. In most cases when a wife is not interested in sex, the cause could be a husband who is ignorant about the problems he causes in bed. However, to resolve this problem, one ought to look beyond sex in the bedroom; he has to look at how he generally relates with his wife. The poor sex life is just a symptom of a bigger problem.

- *Losing respect for the husband*

In some extreme unfortunate cases, it may be surprising to know that an unsatisfied woman may eventually start losing respect for the husband. Of course, this is unexpected among a believing couple. But, as saint Paul admonished, believers are not exempt from this trap if they don't give their sexual life the attention it needs. Satan then takes advantage of the situation by finding a loophole which he uses to provide them with terrible temptations that will eventually destroy their lives – *"Defraud ye not one the other, except it be with consent for a time, that ye may give yourselves to fasting and prayer; and come together again, that Satan tempt you not for your incontinency"* (1 Corinthians 7:5).

Many times when such marital problems manifest in marriage, a man or his wife usually approach an elderly person for counsel. While counselling should always be encouraged as it has helped some people resolve their differences, it is important to note that it many times has also been a futile exercise in handling marital disputes. I am inclined to believe that in marriage, no other person knows the two married persons better than themselves. If the man is not wise enough to discern the real cause of the problem in his marriage, a third party may more likely only add fuel to the fire. If the two individuals cannot be humble enough to each other in trying to resolve their problem, what makes them think one of them will be humble enough to heed the counsel of a third party? In many cases, the intervention from a third party may appear to save the marriage for a while, but with time more tension builds that worsens the situation.

Much of the problems in marriage can be solved by having a healthy communication system. But:

What is communication?

Different people can talk about communication in different ways and with different meanings. For example communication in business has its own technical definition, different from one used by computer experts (for example when they talk about *data communication* which involves the transmission of electronic data). Our area of interest with regards to communication in these lessons on marriage is a different kind of communication; one which is deep and has so many dimensions to it. Some dimension of it do not even involve speaking words. For purposes of this lesson, let us define marriage-communication as:

> *The process of a husband and wife getting to know each other through speaking, fellowshipping and sexual intimacy.*

Let us look at the elements of this definition.

- **Knowing each other**

According to this definition, there is an initial condition of two people not knowing each other and it takes a process of time for the *knowing* to occur. So, the *knowing* is not a one day event but an on-going process. Here is an illustration: as human beings we see each other using the two balls of liquid known as eyes. Using eyes one person can tell the type of outfit the other is wearing including its colour and design. Through sight a person can recognise the other as being either John or Mary. In one sense he can say, *"I know Mary; she is my work-mate."* Although that is knowledge, it is so limited; John does not know the personal side of Mary's life. For example he may not know her favourite food, the type of books she likes to read, and the sort of places she would love to go for a vacation to. Well, if John happens to start working in the same office environment as Mary, and this situation leads them to engage in regular chats together with other officemates, John may begin to know a little more about Mary. Once in a while, say during tea breaks, their conversations may begin to reveal some more details; she may have mentioned something about the food she likes, for example. However, the dimension of knowledge John has of Mary is still shallow. Being a professional work-environment, the other sides of her character may not manifest. So, we can say John is still ignorant of Mary in so many other ways.

Behaviour is something that can be deeply concealed way past a person's nice suit and voice accent, hiding way deep into the heart. It will only take a close person who communicates at the level of the heart to really know what sort of character the other person is. This occurs among a married couple. Even so, however, it may also take considerable time for two married people to fully understand (know) each other completely because some aspects of the heart will only manifest in moments of pain and others during moments of joy; events that may be unevenly spaced in a couple's lifetime.

Signs of danger appear when two people allow situations and circumstances to turn them blind to each other's state of the heart. When differences and misunderstandings grow and begin to shroud one from the other in such a way that one becomes deaf and dumb to the other's needs, communication dies out. Although physically married, the two people have actually become single again, enduring each other's resentments. When the worse comes to the worst, the marriage winds up in divorce. All this makes us understand that divorce is not a one-time event; it started at the time when a couple's communication began to breakdown! A married couple should therefore do all they can to ensure that they are aware of factors that hinder their communication.

Barriers to effective communication in marriage

The following five things must always be avoided; they are a poison which kill a marriage slowly. Whenever you are speaking with your spouse, avoid the following:

- *Lack of empathy*

The word *empathy* means *"the ability to share someone else's feelings or experiences by imagining what it would be like to be in their situation."*[8]

I remember one incident when we were courting with Norah. She had just lost her mobile phone and when we met, she narrated the ordeal. My response was insensitive and without any expression of concern: *"But how could you lose it?"* was all I said as I wanted to bring up another story. I was surprised to see her expression change as she angrily complained: *"You can't even show a little concern?"* When I look back now, I realise how foolish and indifferent I was. My indifferent attitude had much to do with my background: I grew up not knowing what being affectionate meant. It took me long to have a phone. And the first one I had was merely a handset with a sim card. There was almost no difference between owning it and losing it, except for the importance of using text messages and occasional phone-calls which I had to make if I saved a little money to buy airtime which would barely last five minutes. However, being in a relationship required me to learn things that were of concern to my partner but which were not necessarily of any issue to me. In the words of the late Myles Munroe, a great teacher on the subject of marriage:

Marriage is never just the coming together of two people, but a collision of their histories. It is a clash of cultures, experiences, memories, and habits...When you marry someone, you marry more than just a person; you 'marry'...a

---

[8] Cambridge Advanced Learners Dictionary (2008 Edition).

complete history of experiences...Adjusting to these differences is critical to marital survival. Unfortunately, many marriages fail on precisely this point (Munroe, 2002).

When listening to your spouse speaking – whatever the complaint is –learn to think: *"If it was me talking, how would I like to have been treated?"* This thinking process will not only help you to develop empathy but will save you from speaking wrong words which can provoke anger in your spouse. Remember, even right words can be spoken in a wrong way and hence provoke a negative reaction from the person you are speaking to. A wise man is one with the ability to communicate words both in the right way and at an appropriate time. Appropriate time? Yes. I have noticed Norah is quite good at this (and I am slowly learning from her to develop the same virtue in me): When she is not happy about what I said to her, she never responds to me immediately. She will usually be humbly quite as she listens. Then at a time when poor me gets excited and she is also happy, she will cleverly bring up the subject: *"Sweetie, remember that day, I wasn't happy about how you said that; you could have said it better to me."* Her manner of approach makes me humble and apologise to her. It reminds me of the scripture which says, *"A soft answer turneth away wrath: but grievous words stir up anger"* (Proverbs 15:1).

- *Prejudice*

Effective communication can never occur when, as one person is speaking, the other person already has a preconceived idea of why the other person is speaking the way *they* do. As the person is talking you will be planning what to respond to counter what you are being told. Please note that in doing so, you are not listening. So, when answering back, you will not respond to the person talking to you but to your own prejudice. Never be too sure about anything. Listen calmly, giving chance to listen with empathy as your friend is speaking to you.

Prejudice can be caused by various things including what you have heard other people say about your spouse. This can be especially dangerous when the "other people" are your relatives talking ill about your spouse. I have seen this happen to several couples, and this actually happens to be another barrier to communication in marriage.

- *Listening through what your relatives gossip to you about your spouse*

This is one deadly killer of communication in marriage. This happens when a spouse begins to listen to the negative sentiments being spoken about *their* spouse. Such gossip can come from one's parents or siblings. The gossip about a spouse could come in various forms including the relatives' unhappiness about the joblessness of a husband or wife, or the way a husband or wife is perceived as not relating to the other's relatives in a certain expected way. When your ears keep feeding on such negative talk, you gradually begin to look at him/her with three eyes and three ears; trying to observe and sieve words he/she speaks through what you have been hearing from people.

It is a serious error to see your spouse through the distorted prism of what others speak about him or her. Whether certain things other people may speak about your spouse are true, remember that to participate in the negative talk will only make the situation worse and is at best driving nails into your own coffin. Your hubby or wife is not a separate entity from you. Wise people who may want to advise about something in your marriage will be measured in their manner of approach to any problem that affects your marriage; they will be respectful, treat you as one unit, and anything they say or do will be flavoured with the best interest of making your marriage work and not intimidating it into destruction. Unfortunately there are spouses who participate in ill-talk about their partner; it is extremely irresponsible to participate in talk that demeans or ridicules the intelligence of your spouse. Remember that when you finally get in trouble and your marriage becomes shaky, many of the people who may have influenced you to the destruction of your marriage will have little or nothing to assist you with to get on with your life. You will be left alone to tend to your grief. What most people don't realise is that the same people who seem to support you in defaming your spouse would still have never been happy had you been succeeding and prospering with your spouse.

A marriage that relies on outside observers to provide information about its state of affairs is more likely to crumble soon or later. On the converse, a man and woman who got married as true believers, filled with the Holy Spirit, and are mature and serious about their marriage, will spend time in prayer together, attend church and invest in enriching their understanding of marriage through reading relevant books on the subject[9]. Such a couple would know better of what to do when a problem emerges in the home. *First,* they will be humble and sincere with each other. *Second,* because of their godly fear, they will humbly acknowledge a wrong and work to remedy it. The big trouble we have is, many believers are just in *word* but not in *deed.* God is not truly their ultimate authority; ego takes centre stage in the way they act and make decisions. Seeking the Lord and humility are foreign virtues to such couples. Such a state is hopeless and there is little that counselling can do to help.[10] I remember once being

---

[9] It is interesting to note that people spend so much time and countless monies on developing their careers, but yet have little or no time at all to invest in knowledge about the institution in which they will last for a life-time. They are willing to part away with a good number of dollars to buy a text-book or pay school fees; they succeed in their career, getting promotions or having a lucrative business but yet their marriages are failing and falling apart. What vanity!

[10] It is for this reason that I don't give marriage counselling to unbelievers because the basis or standard of their marriage is

approached by a couple who had a problem of serious misunderstandings based on what relatives had been speaking about them. The manner in which the husband talked to the wife and the way she would respond let me know their spirituality was below 'zero degrees Celsius'. Instead of addressing their issue at hand, I decided to put them on 'prayer therapy'. In short time they realised their carnality and the problem was gone. Most problems in many marriages would end with just a little spirituality in a couple. How much more when a couple's heart is entirely given to God; the fullness of the joy of marriage would manifest!

DEAR COUPLE, NEVER ALLOW any event to break down your communication. Don't under-rate a single incident; that single one could form the weakest link in your process of knowing each other. And as the old saying goes, a chain is no stronger than its weakest link. So we don't measure the strength of a chain by examining its strongest links but its weakest ones. When something happens that makes you unhappy at the way *she* said something, or the way *he* treated you. Be calm. Never speak when the other one seems emotional and angry. Always remember that when two people are angry

---

not God's Word. I believe that marriage was instituted by God and the only way it can work right is to measure it up against the standard of God's instructions. The situation of an unbeliever taking his marital problem to a God-believing counsellor is no different from a motorist who takes his faulty car to an aircraft engineer.

and talking, it is not the 'people' talking, it is often infuriated egos at war with each other. The informed person should be calm and be humble as he or she quietly and respectfully listens to the other person's concerns. Humbly telling the offended person, even when you know you are right, *"I am so sorry for hurting you honey; I didn't mean to"*, is not a sign of weakness but maturity. Know that when the other person is angry, nine times out of ten, the chance is that he or she won't listen to, or understand, what you have to say. Your stillness, sincerity and love is what can overcome the fire of fury in the other person. Be the bigger person to handle the situation with love and maturity.

- **Speaking**

A man should express his love for his wife by speaking to her. The wife should also do the same. Do not get tired of telling your spouse:

"You are the best thing that happened to me!"

"When God was making you, He must have been thinking of me!"

"I can't imagine living life without you!"

You don't have to be in the mood of romance for you to communicate these words; you don't have to first have the feeling of love for your spouse before you can send such messages. Do it as a commitment to keep your affection warm in the marriage. It is not much work to take a few seconds off your office desk and make a phone call to tell your wife: *"I have missed you girl!"*

And dear wife, try texting the following words to your husband and see what they will do to him:

> *"I have really missed you My Love, please come home soon after work, I can't wait to have you!"*

As a wife, make your husband know that you enjoy his company, and rather than him always being the one to initiate sex in the bedroom, make days to let him know that you desire him. Such communication will make him happy and love you more.

Dear husband never adopt an attitude of thinking, *"well, my wife knows that I love her; I don't need to tell her or speak such words"*. Believe it or not, she needs to hear you speak out your appreciation and love for her. However, note that the speaking does not have to always be romantic. In fact, communication in mature successful marriages may have very little to do with romance: communication occurs on so many other things about life. To understand this we need to look at the important role of fellowship in a marriage relationship.

• **Fellowship**

As a man you have to understand that a woman's affection for you is not ignited by her ogling at you. While you can get easily aroused by her body-looks, her affection for you is aroused by your attitude and words of love and affection towards her. This is a fundamental difference between males and females that a husband must understand.

When you get off from work, don't just get busy on your computer or phone as you wait for your food to be served. If you can, join your wife in the kitchen; as she washes the dishes help her dry them. Chat about an item you heard on the news or an incident that happened at work. Through such a relationship you will become best friends who will always miss each other's company. You will have moments of chasing each other around like kids. Does, what I have just said sound odd or juvenile? Well, it wasn't odd for Isaac, a patriarch of our Faith: someone once looked outside a window and saw him "*sporting*" (i.e. playing) with Rebekah, his wife (Gen.26:8). If I may ask: when is the last time you did that with your wife?

Now, a chat which may begin with a news item on radio may later turn to become romantic, and later, in the bedroom, consummate into...

• **Sexual intimacy**

A couple with excellent communication often enjoy their sexual life. The speaking and fellowshipping with one another brings them so close together until words stop and hearts in silence begin to mellow out each other. Such a couple are what we can call *soul-mates*; they have met not just at the physical level, but the soul-level, so to speak. The social-glue that binds such persons is unbreakable. The beauty of it is, a couple with such a home many times also happen to raise children who grow up with virtuous lives.

Let me conclude this section on barriers to communication with a story that gives a good illustration of what a barrier in communication can do to two people (the story has gone viral on social media):

A wise man once saw two people shouting in anger at each other. He turned to his disciples and asked:

"Why do people shout in anger at each other?"

There was silence as the disciples thought for a while. Then one of them answered saying:

"Because we lose our calm, we shout."

But to this the wise man asked:

"But, why should you shout when the other person is just next to you? You can as well tell him what you have to say in a soft manner."

The disciples gave one answer after the other but not to the satisfaction of their wise teacher. Finally the teacher explained:

"When two people are angry at each other, their distance between their hearts is far apart. To cover that distance they must shout to be able to hear each other. The angrier they get, the louder they will have to shout to hear each other to cover that great distance. But, what happens when two people fall in love? They don't shout at each other but talk softly, because their hearts are very close. The distance between them is either non-existent or very small. And when they love each other even more, they do not speak but only whisper as they get even closer to each other. Finally they do not even whisper; they only look at each other and that's all. That is how close two people are when they love each other."

The teacher looked at his disciples and said:

"So when you argue do not let your hearts get distant. Do not say words that will cause your hearts to distance from each other; otherwise, there will come a day when the distance is so great that you will not find the path to return. That is how people have ended up in divorce."

I HOPE IT IS now clear why a number of marriages fail; many men, right from the point of entering into marriage, only perceived it as nothing but a platform for satisfying their sexual appetite. However, as we have seen, there is a whole lot that goes with marriage life than just sexual pleasure. Marriage is more about fellowship. This fellowship includes being together and consoling each other in moments of pain, sickness or some other anguish. Actually such sad incidences can even bind a couple more closely in an emotional bond.

The eating analogy of marriage

Being in marriage only for the obsession of sex is like a person who only wants to eat food for the sake of taste. Note that although food, say an orange, may be so tasty in the mouth, its actual work begins after the sweet taste has faded; its work begins when the orange has gone down the gullet into the stomach where it gets digested and eventually provides health when it becomes part of you as blood. Therefore, our drive to eat food is governed by the wider purpose of health and not taste only. People who lack this knowledge often find themselves falling for anything tasty including junk foods which are harmful to health. This clearly is no different from people who find themselves in promiscuous relationships; their sexual appetite craves for and partakes of any *sexy* body they can get a hold of. This is because of the lack of wisdom to see the overall purpose of a man and woman coming together in sexual union. The pleasure that the union provides should not be isolated from the overall and ultimate purpose of the joy of marriage and family. This somewhat strikes a chord with what C.S. Lewis once described:

> *The Christian attitude does not mean that there is anything wrong about sexual pleasure, any more than about the pleasure of eating. It means that you must not isolate that pleasure and try to get it by itself, any more than you ought to try to get the pleasures of taste without swallowing and digesting, by chewing things and spitting them out again* (Lewis, 1944).

To put it in other words, I would say, to experience a healthy marriage one has to look at the big picture.

Have some laughter

It's a Sunday and a man has just returned home from church. Finding his wife relaxing on a sofa he lifts her up, and carries her in his arms as he sings:

"It is well, Oh, it is well with my Soul!"

Astonished and excited, she smilingly asks, as she gives him a peck on the cheek:

"Sweetheart, Did the pastor preach something about love today?"

"Oh, no" he responds:

"He encouraged us to carry our burdens to God in prayer."

3.

The Big Picture

"My first experience on a plane was fascinating; sitting on the window side I watched intently as the plane's wheels detached the ground, closed up into the wheel compartment as it took to the skies. It was amazing to see the once seemingly haphazard big roads thin into tiny well-interconnected geometrical-like lines; the close and isolated vivid greenery transformed into a coherent panoramic view, depicting landscapes with various green and brown shapes of perfect art; the city noise was unheard of in the silence of the sky. My eyes had never seen such a live big picture before!"

A C Phiri

"For which of you, intending to build a tower, sitteth not down first, and counteth the cost, whether he have sufficient to finish it? Lest haply, after he hath laid the foundation, and is not able to finish it, all that behold it begin to mock him, Saying, This man began to build, and was not able to finish"

Luke 14:28-30

Thrill of *'first-time'* things

I remember how I felt when I first ordered my car online; I was so anxious at the thought of starting to drive my own vehicle. When the vehicle finally arrived, the first weeks of being on the steering wheel gave me such a thrill. However, with time, the thrill waned. The excitement vanished, although I still love and take good care of the car. Now, consider this: would it be wise to now think of selling the vehicle simply because I can no longer feel the first thrill of driving? Surely, that would be ridiculous. It would mean missing the purpose of having the car. The car was not bought for the thrill that comes from driving it. It was bought for the purpose of facilitating movements. It is important to understand that although the initial thrill disappeared, an experience which is newer, more stable, inner satisfying and enjoyable, has taken over. The satisfaction and enjoyment comes through the convenience a car provides whenever I want to make movements. That experience can't be traded in with a juvenile first-thrill feeling.

The great philosopher C.S Lewis once explained how the dying of a first-time thrill gives way to a more enduring satisfaction. He illustrated how this is similar to what happens in marriage:

> *People get from books the idea that if you have married the right person you may expect to go on 'being in love' for ever. As a result, when they find they are not, they think this proves they have made a mistake and are entitled to a*

change – not realising that, when they have changed, the glamour will presently go out of the new love just as it went out of the old one. In this department of life, as in every other, thrills come at the beginning and do not last...The thrill you feel on first seeing some delightful place dies away when you really go to live there. Does this mean it would be better not to...live in the beautiful place? By no means...if you go through with it, the dying away of the first thrill will be compensated for by a quieter and more lasting kind of interest...The man who has learned to fly and become a good pilot will suddenly discover music; the man who has settled down to live in the beautiful spot will discover gardening...But if you decide to make thrills your regular diet and try to prolong them artificially, they will get weaker, and fewer and fewer, and you will be a bored, disillusioned old man for the rest of your life. (Lewis, 1944, p.110-111).

Watch his words – "*the dying away of the first thrill will be compensated for by a quieter and more lasting kind of interest*": This is true.

The eating analogy again: when the tasty food is in the mouth, the taste-buds get so entertained that one may want to chew the nice food forever. However, the experience only lasts for a few seconds. But, the real purpose of the food actually begins after it has dropped through the gullet, down into the stomach. Satisfaction – the feeling of being *full* and energetic occurs when the food is in the stomach. It is in the stomach where the important process of digestion begins. This process further leads to the food slowly being absorbed into you, becoming blood. Notice here that these two processes - *satisfaction* and *digestion* – are not like the noisy, charming and entertaining processes of *chewing* and *tasting* which occur in the mouth; they are *quiter* but yet produce more *lasting* results than taste. So, for a man who only eats for the sake of taste, and disregards the proper choice of healthy food, his appetite will always lead him to more appealing and scrumptious junk foods (which are designed to entertain taste buds but very poisonous to the body). The way of a gluttonous person is *momental* taste but eventual disease and death. Isn't this the same way people who only marry for the sake of beauty and sexual feelings end up?

"Love" or "Feelings of Love"?

People who only marry for beauty and for the thrill of love often find themselves wondering: "*Why has this happened; we were once in love with my spouse but now everything has changed!*" Well, it may not really be that love has diminished. True love is enduring. The common problem people make is to mistake *love* for what Bruce and Carol Britten call *"feelings of love"* (Britten and Britten, 2003):

> *The 'feeling of love' is not the same as 'love'. What is the' feeling of love'? It's the exciting feeling of, 'She loves me, and I love her.' Million songs have been written about this marvellous feeling. Yet, few people understand that even in a good marriage, the feeling of love rises...falls...rises...falls.*
>
> *Today a husband may have a strong feeling of love for his wife, but tomorrow that feeling may fall...the next day it may rise...but soon after that it may fall...and later rise again. Why? Because the feeling of love is just a feeling, and our feelings always change.*
>
> *We humans have many different feelings. Sometimes we feel angry, sometimes lonely, and sometimes we feel in love. We don't have the same feeling every day. Have you ever felt happy every day for a month? No, happiness is a feeling and so it comes and goes. All feelings rise, fall, rise...And that includes the feeling of love. (p.18-19).*

The sooner a couple understands the difference between "*love*" and "*feelings of love*" the better they will understand and manage their emotional swings.

What is love? It is *that* deep affection, attachment and appreciation one has for his or her spouse. When *he* looks at her, he sees a life-long companion that he has to work hard for to ensure she is healthy, protected and happy. And when *she* looks at him, she sees an inspiration, her leader, a protector, a provider and one who understands her emotional needs of sympathy and empathy.

Loving a person does not mean he or she is perfect; it involves being aware of, and accommodating, your spouse's shortcomings. In the excellent book *SECRETS OF FASCINATING WOMANHOOD*,[11] a book that teaches lessons on how a wife can make her marriage happy, David Coory (the author) has this advice for wives: accept your husband *"as another human being, part good, part bad, just like yourself"* (Coory, 2009,p.31). This is true because part of the nature of love is *acceptance,* just like the way God accepted us in the state we were in when we came to Him as sinners. He forgave our sins and that expression of love for mankind makes any person who has understood it to also love God in return.

These characteristics of love in marriage are not just based on feelings of the flesh; they entail an enduring commitment which is grounded in what a person is to you – *the flesh of your flesh*. This love does not get affected when *Jane* arrives late and *Peter* gets angry for her usual poor time-keeping habits. They can angrily talk over it, but they know that the little thing which has happened has nothing to do with their bond of love. That thing called *love* is still intact, way deep inside their hearts. It is so deep that the outward fluctuations of emotions don't affect it; misunderstandings are

---

[11] This is a highly recommended book for married women. It is available for download on: www.fascinatingwomanhood.co.nz.

dealt with as misunderstandings in themselves and not as links to their bond of love. In such a mature relationship, people will be seen laughing together even a few minutes after arguing over why *she* was late, or why *he* didn't do what *she* had requested for. Unfortunately this is not what we see in many marriages; a simple argument soon winds up in such talk like "*You don't love me!*" It is scary and dangerous when love always gets questioned whenever a couple have a petty argument. Such a marriage has a very shaky foundation.

Feelings of love, as explained by Bruce and Carol Britten above, are intermittent passions or thrills of excitement one may experience for his spouse. The thrills may often lead to a couple embracing each other. The trouble is, feelings of love, unlike love itself, fluctuate. One cannot experience them all the time. And the sad reality for couples whose marriages survive on the feelings of love is that, the longer a couple lives together in marriage, the less frequent they experience thrills. This occurs both in successful and non-successful marriages. However, there is a difference in the way the fluctuations of emotions of love are interpreted in successful and non-successful marriages: in successful marriages they are correctly interpreted for what they are – fluctuating emotions! And in unsuccessful marriages they are taken to mean the *presence* or *the absence of love*. This misconception has led some people to divorce and to re-marry several times.

The fluctuations or fading of *"feelings of love"* is not a problem for a wise and mature couple. The couple understands that when the youthful excitement wanes, there is actually something that has happened to them which has made them to become truly one until they don't see their separateness. What they now have is the joy of *fellowship, companionship* and *friendship* – valuables which are not easily replaceable. The stronger the social-glue the more lasting a marriage becomes. When a marriage is at such a level of maturity what triggers excitement in the husband or wife to have sex is not mere sight or infatuation, but love on a deeper level. One husband's narration of his experience (found in Dr Cox's book, *HUMAN INTIMACY*) is worth noting here. It is about changes in sexual-life which he has gone through with his wife in the fifteen years they have been married:

> *I find that after fifteen years of marriage the quality of our sex life has increased immensely even as the quantity has decreased. Sex between us seems to serve as a bonding agent...*
>
> *Like most young men, I was attracted to her physical attractiveness, her smile, her body...and other physical qualities and these attributes still attract me. Today, however, I can take a shower with her and not necessarily become sexually aroused. I couldn't event imagine such a thing at the start of our relationship. A tiny glimpse of her*

nude and I was turned on. If seeing her nude does not necessarily turn me on today, what does?

We take a ski trip with the children. I watch them happily skiing down the hill with grace and skill...she is the mother of these wonderful children. She bore them and cared for them and helped (along with me, I hope) to make them what they are. I admire and respect her and love her and want to tell her this. What better way to communicate this than to physically get close to her, feel her, share our love together?... I think of the things she really doesn't like about me but tolerates and accepts. I think about her encouragement when I tried something new or difficult. And suddenly I am sexually attracted to her and want to hold and cuddle her and tell her 'thank you.'

Of course, we have sex for sex. Of course, we have sex when there is no time, when we can't concentrate. But then there are times when our souls meet, when sex becomes the ultimate communication, when it stands for all the things she means to me, when it transcends all our differences, all our problems, when it becomes the ultimate expression of our love...

Of course, I'm attracted to other women at times. Of course, the sexual excitement is sometimes missing, but I wouldn't trade in our sex life. After all, it took years to build it into a meeting of our souls. Would I really trade that in on a one-night stand because I was horny? No way! (Cox, 2002, p.247).

There are three important facts to note in this man's story:

- With time, the *quantity* of sex in a marriage can decrease while its *quality* increases. This point should let us become aware of the following fact:

- Quantity of sex *does* not always imply quality-sex. So, it is possible for a couple to be having lots of sex but which lack the quality of their souls meeting. Such a sexual life will not contribute to the joy of marriage.

- Quality-sex develops over a period of time and is a process that brings two people to become 'soul-mates'. This quality-sex becomes an important fabric in the texture of the social-glue that binds a couple.

The value of the social glue that develops between spouses is irreplaceable. It takes a long time to flourish and once blemished or desecrated by acts of infidelity, its original flavour can never be restored. However, if a man and woman sincerely love each other, they will not live in fear of suspecting each other of dirty secret behaviour.

Their *"perfect love"* does not give any place to fear (cf. 1 John 4:18).[12]

Now, let us not be mistaken to think that any marriage of many years is a successful one.

Holes in the wall

A few years back I came to learn that being in marriage for so many years is not always a sign of love between a husband and wife; some long-enduring marriages are actually a form of *life imprisonment* where a husband and wife have cleaved together, not out of love but, because circumstances have compelled them to do so.

It was during a visit to India when I was approached by an elderly man. He was probably in his mid or late sixties. He was in a bad shape being troubled by a chronic disease which gave him difficulties in speaking. I patiently sat still, listened as he bitterly complained about the lack of care and respect his children showed him as a head of the family. He asked me to pray for him so that God could bring joy in his marriage and family. After his lengthy explanation I decided to ask him:

---

[12] However, what would be very dangerous is when one spouse perceives perfect love in their marriage but when the other spouse is actually a cheating hypocrite with extra-marital affairs. I have handled counselling sessions where one spouse was not only a hypocrite but a very skilled and sophisticated one. It can be a very traumatising and painful experience when the cheated spouse discovers the truth.

"*Have you ever discussed this problem with your pastor?*"

"*No. My pastor is not capable of handling this problem*", he answered. To that I said:

> "*Well, there are many other details I may not know about your problem and what may have led to your sad current state of affairs. I am a stranger here and your pastor should be in a better position to advise you.*"

I then proceeded to ask him:

> "*Before you fell ill; the time when you had strength and a job to fend for your family; did they find in you a man they could truly call their daddy; a man who could find time to care, inspire, and love them?*"

At that point he kept quite; seemingly looking uncomfortable with the question. Then he confessed:

> "*I made mistakes; I wasn't there for my wife and my children; actually my wife has laboured so much in providing for the family that I don't want to bother her anymore. I didn't live right, but you see, I have been telling my wife that all that is now in the past and we need to look at the present and future.*"

I felt sorry for the man; he had offended his family and he was now desperate for a visiting minister to pray over the matter. He probably was hoping that I would also summon and admonish his family. I could not do that. Dear couple listen to this; there could be incidental mistakes a person can make to his or her spouse; forgiveness can occur and life made to go on. However, when one develops a habit of doing wrong the damage caused can be irreparable. In such a situation, saying sorry may be easy but it would be like trying to remove nails which you had earlier forced through a wall; although you can manage to remove and throw them away, the ugly dent they leave behind will still remain. Bad words, wrong behaviour and attitudes can create mistrust and disharmony which can be difficult to heal. The Scripture admonishes – *"make straight paths for your feet, lest that which is lame be turned out of the way; but let it rather be healed"* (Hebrews 12:13).[13]

Seeking counsel from visiting ministers

While some couples have been helped by counsel offered by visiting ministers, many times it does not occur that way.

There are always people in a local church who often get so excited at the preaching of a visiting

---

[13] If your marriage is in a critical condition, there could still be a chance for it to be restored. Make efforts to get the book *ANSWERS FOR YOUR MARRIAGE* by Bruce and Carol Britten (Britten and Britten, 2003). This book has transformed many marriages and is one of the top recommended texts used at Believers Assembly's counselling sessions for about-to-be-married couples. It is available on www.amazon.com.

minister that they would desire to seek audience with him and ask for counsel about some problems they are going through in their lives. Unknown to the minister, the person seeking counsel may have approached various other pastors who visited the church.   Unfortunately some pastors are too sanguine and careless and go about offering counsel and prayers without understanding the intricacies which could have led to the problem the person is going through.[14] Let us give heed to Saint Paul's admonition to Timothy to *"lay hands suddenly on no man, neither be partaker of other men's sins: keep thyself pure"* (1 Timothy 5:21-22).

A minister, or any other person in a position to offer counsel, should beware that marital problems are often a nexus of many convoluted factors which develop over time. A counsellor will need a *third eye* to understand underlying issues. Offering counsel haphazardly to any stranger that comes to you can sometimes lead to more problems especially when a person being counselled starts to use your words as an authority and defence for their wrong behaviour which you could not witness during your short visit. Beware, there are many people who take *authority for truth* instead of *truth for authority.*

---

[14] When on foreign missionary work, I have never found it wise to conduct counselling sessions unless the pastor of a local church has requested me to do so, or if it is a minister himself in need of (and has requested for) the counselling.

The money problem

Sometime in the year 2011 I was in Kampala, the capital city of Uganda. After preaching in a church service, a short, stout, very talkative but cheerful man came to me, extending his hand to greet me. I reached forth and we exchanged greetings. He then began praising me for the "powerful sermon!" At the end of his eulogy he showed me a dry scar on his head, as he explained:

> *This scar was as a result of a bad injury I had on my head. I can't do very hard work now because of the injury I had. I now need to get married but I don't have the money to pay dowry and to start a new home. Would you help me please?*

Although the man called the preaching "*powerful*", I doubt if he could remember even two words of the sermon he heard; his purpose of coming to me was not to appreciate the sermon but to ask for money. However my important concern was if he really understood what marriage entailed. If he is now married and still has the same mind-set of thinking that someone could jump-start him into a better life which would enable him to marry, then I am afraid his wife and children are most likely in problems.

Strange as the Ugandan man's request seemed, there are actually many people who enter marriage with the same attitude; they have the same mind-set only to a varying degree. Many people get into marriage, and live through marriage, without having a sound financial plan.

There are many men who foolishly live a care-free life, moving about as busy-bodies, without a job or plan of how to make a living. *"The Lord shall provide"* is often their lame excuse. If you want to marry or are already a married man and this is your behaviour, someone has hard words for you:

If you're having money problems before you are married, what makes you think they will go away after you are married? The time to think about finances is before the wedding – long before. A couple should discuss the matter frankly and honestly and have a clear financial plan in place before they take their vows...No woman, even if she has her own career and plans to continue working should marry a man who does not have a job. If she does, she will most likely end up supporting him, rather than the other way around. (Munroe, 2002, p.67).

Someone may feel that Munroe is too harsh. Well, the scriptures seem harsher:

Neither did we eat any man's bread for nought; but wrought with labour and travail night and day, that we might not be chargeable to any of you...If any would not work, neither should he eat. For we hear that there are some which walk among you disorderly, working not at all, but are busybodies. Now them that are such we command and exhort by our Lord Jesus Christ, that with quietness they work, and eat their own bread. (2 Thessalonians 3:7-12).

These are important words, especially for a man contemplating marriage. One should never be overtaken by thoughts of "*We are in love.*" While it is true that two people can be in love, they also need to consider the livelihood of children who will come through their union. There is need for them to carefully plan on how they intend to survive financially when they get married. Here we are not talking about a person becoming very rich or getting a high paying job before he marries; we are talking about the need for a man to be resourceful and responsible enough to work and take care of his wife. It may not be a high paying job, or not a big business, that one has, but the bottom line is that he should be a person with direction and the ability to sustain a woman whom he has decided to bring into his life.

Married but dependents

There is nothing more embarrassing and inappropriate than getting married but being still dependent on your parents for your livelihood. In the first place, as was explained in the introduction, marriage involves *leaving the house of your parents.* That entails being totally independent in terms of financial sustenance and decision making.

It is amazing to know that there are some couples who depend on their parent's support for livelihood. In some more unfortunate circumstances, there are some young men who upon failing to keep up with rent and food expenses would resort to letting the wife stay with her parents with the hope of getting her back when circumstances get better. Now, no matter how the parents can seem welcoming and smiling in offering their assistance, that is simply a ridiculous thing for a man to do. Even if someone's parents were very rich, a married man who fails to make ends meet and decides to take shelter under them simply lacks common sense and he was not mature enough to get into marriage in the first place; he may have grown in stature and height but not in wisdom. Such a young man most likely got into marriage with a limited view ('small picture') of romance and not having understanding of the bigger issues of the overall commitment and independence that come with marriage.

If a man is not man enough to stand on his two feet in times of adversity, he should not have a wife because another human coming to lean on him will only lead to an embarrassing great fall. On the converse, if a man is poor but yet has enough resilience and focus, then a wife would be safe in his hands. This reminds me of an incident Rev. Branham once narrated about a young man and woman who approached him to sanction their marriage: the young couple looked very poor. He narrates:

And I said, "You love this girl?"
He said, "Yes, sir. I do."
I said, "You love him?"
Yes, sir. I do."
I said, "I want to ask you something. I understand, you're working up here on this P.W.A."
And he said, "Yes, sir." That's about twelve dollars a week.
I said, "You think you can make a living for her?"
He said, "I'll do all I can do."
And I said, "Well, that's all right."
(Branham, 1965)

Basic roles of a husband in a home

A husband's basic roles in a home include:

- *Providing the basic necessities for the family.*

This includes money, food and other forms of nourishment that will make his family alive and healthy. This is a primary responsibility of a husband, not a wife. Although a woman may also be engaged in employment, a man should still show leadership as the provider of the home; a woman's efforts should only be a supplement.

- *Preparing, with the wife, the financial plan for the future of their family.*

Failing to prepare is preparing to fail, so the old saying states. Some believers foolishly take faith to mean walking through life carelessly without any plan, hoping for God to take care of the future. This terrible mind-set of doing things anyhow, without a plan, has led to marriages of some Christian couples end up with very large numbers of children whom they cannot adequately support. This is done in the name of fulfilling God's commission to multiply and fill the earth. Well, it's about time someone knew that the earth is already full and the United Nations organisation is actually having a hard time to educate people about controlling population growth. One thing is certain; the lack of knowledge, especially in poor Third World countries has destroyed a lot of lives. (More about this in the next chapter).

- *Providing inspiring leadership in a home which should enable and inspire children to grow up into responsible and prosperous adults.*

Life is hard; we live in a tough indifferent world. As believers, the Lord admonished us to be aware that although we are in this world we are not of this world. Our purpose is not in the pursuit of riches for the sake of it; we have a hope and a life beyond this present sin-sick world. However, all things being normal, a believer should work to ensure that the economic future of his children is secured. He should work to ensure that they eat healthy and get a good education. One thing is certain, if these basic necessities are not met, the child will grow up facing the ugly side of this world – poverty, diseases, and the inability to access proper medical care. These things really matter. It is true that God has helped certain poor people in certain miraculous ways but we also know that God doesn't do miracles anyhow and at any time. Whilst having faith is very important, we also have a responsibility to efficiently use the resources he has provided us with. The most important natural resource God gave a human being is the brain through which the mind operates. Use it wisely and you will prosper; use it poorly and you will be so disadvantaged. A husband and father at home should inspire children to make full use of their God-given abilities. A husband together with his wife ought to be the best friend and mentor to the children. This doesn't necessarily require a parent to be educated. An uneducated parent can still inspire children to education. Today we have the *"Ben Carson Story"* – a true legendary story of a man who was raised by a poor uneducated black American woman who couldn't read or write and could only raise income as a maid. She realised the importance of reading and education and emphasised this to her children. Out of those efforts came the world's renowned paediatric neurosurgeon, a God-fearing man who has saved countless lives of children. That would never have been possible if that poor woman didn't take a bold step to inspire her children to achieve what she failed to.

Mrs Carson was concerned about the future of her children; she stopped them from being obsessed with watching TV (a one-eyed monster that I believe is keeping a lot of African children dull!); she disciplined her children to get into a reading lifestyle. I should emphasise that Mrs Carson was concerned about the future of her children! She knew how they would end-up if their school grades were poor or if all they could think of was watching the next TV comedy programme. On the other hand she knew what kind of a bright future awaited if only the children could do what other successful people in society were doing. Sadly, we don't have many parents like that. Many men and women who get married live life as a series of meaningless disconnected unplanned events; it seems their eyes can only see as far as what is before them; they have never awaken to the deep thought about life, its meaning, and what role them and their children ought to play in it. Life is a great drama and you ought to play your part right. Someone said that you only live once, but when you do it right, once is enough.

To live right one should first consider the overall picture of life and think about where they are, what the various events surrounding them mean, and map out a way of where they intend to be. Looked at this way, life will cease to be haphazard. Even your routine activities will take on fresh meaning as the enthusiastic you begin to invest more passion and energy into your work, hoping to reach your desired end. This reminds me of my first time on a plane: it was fascinating; sitting on the window side I watched intently as the plane's wheels detached the ground, closed up into the wheel compartment as it took to the skies. It was amazing to see the once seemingly haphazard big roads thin into tiny well-interconnected geometrical lines; the close and isolated vivid greenery transformed into a coherent panoramic view, depicting landscapes with various green and brown shapes of perfect art; the city noise was unheard of in the silence of the sky. My eyes had never seen such a live big picture!

Have some laughter

After a long winded sermon, the preacher looked at the expectant audience as the bride and groom stood before him. He asked:

"Is there anyone in the audience who knows anything about the groom or the bride that should   stop us from proceeding to marry them?"

Solemn silence ensued but which was soon interrupted when the reverend saw a hand of an elderly man raised at the back of the building.

"Yes please, you can speak sir!"

Immediately the groom took to the door at lightning speed. The bride fainted. The audience sighed. And the elderly man, who hadn't noticed the drama, spoke:

"Reverend, We can't hear you from the back, kindly speak louder!"

4.
See afar

"Art is long, and time is fleeting,
And our hearts, though stout and brave,
Still, like muffled drums, are beating
Funeral marches to the grave"

Henry W. Longfellow

"Let thine eyes look right on, and let thine eyelids
look straight before thee. Ponder the path of thy
feet, and let all thy ways be established. Turn not
to the right hand nor to the left"

Psalm 4:25-27

See afar

It is important to realise that a person's life should not be a series of meaningless, haphazard, and disconnected series of events. Life should be guided by certain goals and ideals that a person has been convinced to be worth living for. Furthermore, everything a person aspires for should be in congruence with the identified goals. It goes without saying that marriage is one place where a person has to go high up in his mind and perceive the big picture of the *past, present* and *future.* The past because it is important to draw a pattern and interpretation of how past events have culminated into the present situation. A person who is so obsessed with daily routine life that he or she does not have time to pause and evaluate their lifestyle is bound to live a life of doing same things over and over again, yet hoping that something somehow will change for the better one day. Albert Einstein had a word for that; he said that doing the same thing over and over again and expecting different results is *insanity*!

By examining the past and present state of his or her life, a person can go through an introspection of what they need to change in order to be a better person tomorrow. We need to understand that time is a finite resource; each tick of a second takes you closer to your grave. Your heart-beat is a 'timer' which is ticking to the count of your life; like a muffled drum, it is beating your funeral march to the grave. I love this expression in Longfellow's *Psalm of Life*:

> *Art is long, and time is fleeting,*
> *And our hearts, though stout and brave,*
> *Still, like muffled drums, are beating*
> *Funeral marches to the grave.*

Quite a solemn poem.

Number your days!

If you are a parent and are reading this and you have a child old enough to start school, ask yourself these questions:

1. *How old will I be the time my child completes his secondary school?*

2. *By then, will I have enough income to manage my child's college or university expenses?*

3. *By then, will I have enough energy, to work so hard? If not, what investments can I make now that will enable me, in the future, to generate income that will cater for my children's education's expenses?*

4. *How are my eating habits and do I do enough exercises to keep myself healthy? Does the kind of food I eat put me at risk of having diabetes, hypertension, or obesity?*

5. *What would happen if I die before my child completes school? Do I have investments which can secure my child's future?*

These are not pleasant questions to answer but they will help you a lot if you give them even a little attention. And, if the many people in Africa and other Third World regions of the world were to take time to ask themselves these pertinent questions, we would not have the problem of fathers with overly large families which they fail to support financially. Consider the following fictitious case that will help us answer the above five questions:

There is a *Mr Tembo* who is 30 years old at the time of answering *question 1* above. He has a child named *Peter* who has just started grade one. Mr Tembo has a job that doesn't pay so well and hardly ever meets his regular expenses such as house rent and groceries (not mentioning the incessant financial requests that come from his siblings, parents, and in-laws). In addition, Peter's school fees are a knew expense to his budget. How will he live his life (with regards to the questions above) in the course of managing the education expenses of Peter? In my country of Zambia it takes 12 years for one to complete the primary and secondary school levels of education. So, for a Zambian Mr Tembo, answers to the questions above can be illustrated as follows:

1. *30 years (his age) + 12 years (duration of primary and secondary school for his child) = 42 years old.*

So, Mr Tembo will be 42 years old at the time Peter is completing his secondary school. Let us hope that in 12 years' time Mr Tembo's income would have rose enough to cover Peter's university education. However, if Mr Tembo is very relaxed with his current job and only hopes for a promotion or luck to find a better job in the future, he is surely headed for trouble. If he does not take time to stop, think, analyse, and evaluate his current state of affairs and plan ahead, he is destined to end up as a disgruntled old man who will become a burden to his own children, and will often get stressed with many pressures of life.

What Mr Tembo needs to realise is that the job he so much cherishes today may not be there tomorrow. The question he needs to seriously ponder on is, *"What will happen to me, my wife, and children if this steady flow of income were to stop?"* It is highly unlikely that Mr Tembo can start and build a successful business when he is old. As I am writing this, I know of one old poor man who suddenly has decided to become an entrepreneur at the age of 83. Much as we should appreciate such enthusiasm, I know the man to have once had a steady income but for which he never took care of the needs of his family; to-date there is literary no single property he can point at which he has left for his children. Today he constantly asks for money from his children who have very little attachment with him. What is more, some of his children seem to be still grieved at the uncaring attitude he exhibited towards the family when he used to have money. I wonder how far his entrepreneurship venture will take him as I gather that a successful business usually takes about ten years to build (and this would definitely be done best when a person is in his prime age of life).

2. *Mr Tembo is now 42 years old and his child has to be in college. Well, let us assume that he still has his job at the same company. However, he is now more stressed than ever before because he now has two more children, John and Mary, who are in primary school.*

The two children will require a schedule of their own for this calculation we are making. If Mr Tembo is now 42, his second born, John, is 11 years old and in grade five, and the youngest, Mary, is 7 years old and in grade one. This means that Mr Tembo will be 54 years old at the time of Mary completing her secondary school. The troublesome question is: where will Mr Tembo gather resources to simultaneously manage the accumulating expenses of the three children? Take note that this example is over-simplified; if we consider other expenses such as house rent, water and electricity bills, food budget, and other miscellaneous expenses, it is more likely that Mr Tembo may become a victim of high blood pressure and other such illnesses associated with stress; he certainly will have to endure an unhappy depressing life. Now, although what we have analysed this far should be burdensome enough for a father of three, imagine a typical Zambian father of seven, eight, or nine children: just what kind of life do they have?

When people find themselves in such stressful situations it is common to find them constantly requesting for prayer, and moving from one *altar-call* to another in the hope of finding a miracle from God. Much as I believe in divine healing and miracles, I am also inclined to believe that God does not take care of careless; most of the problems people are going through were self-created at a time when they had opportunities to do the right thing. Think of Mr Tembo: are his problems really caused by some *"demon of poverty"* or *"witchcraft spells"*? Aren't they simply a result of the lack of knowledge (i.e. ignorance)? Let us give heed to the admonition from Scripture: *"My people are destroyed for lack of knowledge: because thou hast rejected knowledge, I will also reject thee"* (Hosea 4:6).

3. *At 42 or 54, Mr Tembo will not be as energetic as he used to be!*

One of the things that robs people of their energy as they get older is the ill-health that often develops with old-age. The ill-health incapacitates a person from living an active lifestyle. However, in many cases, this is something that can be controlled or avoided if a person, whilst young, is health-conscious and has a sound financial life. Having a sound financial life does not mean having millions of dollars; one can have a simple salary or business income which he conscientiously manages through careful planning. In the Tembo case we are looking at, the lack of financial resources will affect Mr Tembo in a lot of ways:

- *He will not have time to do exercises as he will be preoccupied with a lot of stressful activities in the hope of generating extra income. During his old age he may find himself still working as an employee for a meagre salary. Mr Tembo will not avoid this situation as there are many children depending on him.*

- *He will not have money to afford a regular well-balanced diet.*

- *When his health begins to break down he will not afford the ever rising cost of good medical care.*

In one *Believers' Couples Fellowship* meeting I remember seeing the fear in the faces of couples as taught on these matters, admonishing them to be *"wise as serpents, and harmless as doves."*[15]

4. *Much of Mr Tembo's routine diet includes carbohydrate rich foods such as cereals. His breakfast mainly consists of bread and tea, or rice. Mr Tembo has never thought of exercising. It is just something which has never been on his mind.*

---

[15] Matthew 10:16

There is a big problem here. Of course Mr Tembo doesn't see the problem because his body seems to be working fine without feelings of illness. What he doesn't know however is that the imbalance between his high intake of carbohydrates and bodily exercises are slowly building a fatal condition in his body which will only manifest when he will be in his middle age. He is dying slowly without knowing it! If Mr Tembo is aware of the consequences of his bad lifestyle but yet always postpones changing to a healthy lifestyle, then he is committing a slow-paced suicide.

It is unfortunate that most traditional counselling lessons which aim to prepare new couples for marriage do not give attention to these weightier matters; much emphasis seems to be placed on matters of sexuality. As has been discussed this far, there are many other crucial things that the new husband and wife need to be taught. One such thing is a lesson on the importance of adopting a health-conscious lifestyle in a home. As you may already be aware there are many homes which have been robbed of the joy of marriage by illness. Please remember that health problems not only bring about the stress from medical bills but they can also destroy a couple's sexual life. For example, diseases like diabetes or hypertension often lead to *erectile dysfunction* (i.e. impotence) in men; this is a condition where a man fails to maintain an erection during sexual intercourse. There are different causes of diabetes and among them is living a bad lifestyle of not eating healthy and the lack of regular body exercises (see **Appendix I** - *Diseases that can affect a couple's sexual life*).

5. *"Mr Tembo has died!" The sad news has been announced.*

His relatives and siblings will shed tears and express their *"heart-felt"* condolences for the bereavement, but the reality is that no one will give the deceased's children the same love, attention, and affection as he would have. If Mr Tembo has died at a time when all the three children are young and still in school, their future is more likely to be jeopardised, and of the three, Mary, being a girl, may be the most vulnerable. On the other hand, if Peter completed his college education and has a job at the time of his father's death, he is more likely to inherit the commitment of taking care of his siblings. Although Peter can be commended for being a responsible young man who has shown maturity in taking care of his siblings, when we look at the big picture we will soon notice the many ways the untimely death of his father will negatively affect his potential for a successful life. If Peter decides to marry, his wife will be married to a man who is already tied with responsibilities of a father of two. Financial strain and stress will be unavoidable in the home of the new couple. The situation may be further worsened by financial requests which will gradually start coming from Peter's in-laws. It is highly unlikely that when the time comes for the couple's children to start school they will go to a good one. In most poor countries schools with excellent educational facilities are a reserve for those who are ready to part away with good amounts of money.

Now, having described all the potential problems Peter is likely to face, following the demise of his father, what do you think would be the situation if he gets to have a large family of about five or six children? This would more likely lead to a vicious cycle of poverty.

One day a janitor came to my office to pay back some money he had owed me for some time. He began by telling me the number of problems he had experienced in that month:

> *"My child had gone out to play and he ended up injuring himself and so I had to use some money for his medicals. Shortly after that my wife's labour pangs started and this happened at a time I was so broke. But she now delivered and we are now fine so I have decided to come and give you the money owed".*

After telling him I was sorry for what happened, I curiously asked:

"How many children do you have now?"

"Six!" came the resounding answer. I was stunned because the man looked young.

"Six?" I exclaimed.

Quickly realising that my astonishment was explicit I tried to re-compose my calm but then came the defensive response:

> *"Yes I have six children; the commandment to procreate was given by God as written in the Bible!"*

After the man gave me the amount he owed, the usual burden and frustration I have always had concerning people's ignorance about the importance of planning settled on my mind that afternoon. I wondered to myself;

> *Here I am; I have two children for whom I am making savings and investments, and I have decided to take them to a good school for which I am struggling to manage the tuition fees. Whenever a problem of sickness comes up, going to a public clinic has always been frustrating and time-wasting as there are too few staff to attend to the too numerous patients in sub-standard, over-populated, and unkempt wards. The high-cost medical facilities we have signed up for with my wife are expensive but worthwhile. But now, how does this poor man, employed only as a sweeper, with a salary way lower than mine, manage his family of six? What kind of schools do they go to? What happens when they are sick? What kind of a future will they have? Suppose their father dies, what will happen to them?*

Let us understand that much of the problems of insufficiency can be avoided if one can be committed to making good use of the gift of *free will* which God has endowed on mankind. One can use free will to develop, to deprive, or even to destroy himself or herself and other people under their care.

How many children do you see?

THERE ARE MANY THINGS a person can change about their circumstances by simply beginning to make right decisions. One important decision you will ever make in life is to learn how to number your days. Like the ancient Hebrew psalmist, we ought to pray for God to *"teach us to number our days, that we may apply our hearts unto wisdom"* (Psalm 90:12).

A person who wakes up to the reality of how our earthly time is finite will be stirred to start seeking wisdom concerning how best they can live a fruitful life. This awakening can inspire a person to start regarding time like other finite resources. Finite resources like food or money deplete, and so does time. When someone gets his salary and does not treat it as a finite resource, he is bound to spend it carelessly. It will only be a matter of days when he will realise that only a few pennies are remaining. One thing we can be sure of is that no amount of prayers will restore his salary because God doesn't provide subsidy for ignorance. It is for this reason that preparing a budget is a well-known activity among people. Money is a limited resource and it just ought to be planned for! So, why should someone not plan time, a far more important resource? Time is one resource which is non-renewable and on which all other resources depend (See **Appendix II** - *Benefits of planning*).

Family planning

Scheduling of time and finances should form the core aspects of family planning. Unfortunately what comes to many people's minds when the word *"family planning"* is mentioned is the swallowing of contraceptive pills and how to *space* children. Please notice that these are not processes of planning but mechanisms for implementing family planning. Family planning should be broader in concept; it can be defined as *the process of thinking carefully and deciding about how a family can be effectively managed in order to achieve or secure its prosperous future.* This responsibility lies squarely on the shoulders of a father and mother of a family unit. The two should ponder carefully over the decisions they intend to make - "*Let thine eyes look right on, and let thine eyelids look straight before thee. Ponder the path of thy feet, and let all thy ways be established. Turn not to the right hand nor to the left*" (Psalm 4:25-27).

Family planning should involve the following:

- Planning with your spouse about how many children you intend to have.

- Planning about the kind of education you want for your children.

- Calculating your family's regular expenses, comparing them against how much you earn, noting the difference, and planning how to eliminate the deficit.

- Planning the kinds of medical schemes and insurance to invest in.

- Planning when you are going to retire.

Let us look at each of the above items in detail.

1. *Planning with your spouse about how many children you intend to have.*

Some believers feel this is not right because life comes from God. This argument is quite flawed and uninformed. Think about this: when Eve gave birth to Cain she exclaimed, *"I have gotten a man from the LORD"* (Genesis 4:1); do these words mean that it is God who told Eve to conceive Cain? Not so. But that the process of reproduction that leads to the conception of life are based on natural laws which were created by God. Conception is initiated by acts of free will but is guided by God's established natural laws; it takes free will for couples to copulate and laws of reproduction only take over to guide the process of conception.

The law of reproduction follows that if a sperm meets with an egg, fertilisation will occur which will lead to conception. This law cannot be changed; it will still work whether a sexual act has occurred through fornication or within the right confines of marriage. However, it is up to the human beings to use their free will to reason, choose, and decide about *when* to conceive. Otherwise, if one thinks it to be *faith* to always act according to the natural impulses working in his body, only time can tell what abnormal size of a family he will end up having. One thing is certain; he will be enjoying the pleasure of intercourse but whilst putting in danger the many lives of children that he won't be able to adequately take care of (read **Appendix III** – *"I will multiply thy conception"*).

2. *Planning for the kind of education you want for your children.*

School plays an important role in determining the kind of future a child will have. When a child is born, he or she has joined human society. Right from the time of birth he or she needs to be oriented to the way society operates. Human society has a long history in which it has evolved; from simple beginnings to the current complex state.

The changes that occur in society seem to be dictated by the ever versatile needs of mankind: at one time human survival only depended on looking for food in the wild. This was the *hunter-gatherer age* in which a person who knew how to hunt and gather food survived. If you did not have the skill you died. Then later came the *agrarian age* when, instead of always hunting for animals, man became smarter by domesticating them. In addition to that, man also learned to plant crops in his nearby surroundings. This change required owning land. Some people quickly adapted to the change and began to own large portions of land. They became the rich. Others could not see or interpret the change of time and hence found themselves working for the rich. These became the poor. Hundreds of years afterwards, the need for work to be done faster led men to start mechanising equipment. This began in Britain. Hand tools were replaced with power-driven machines. For example the manual process of weaving cloth was mechanised using the *power loom*, and the *steam engine* was invented which enabled steamboats and locomotives to move faster. This, in history, is known as the *industrial age.* It was a great time of invention. However, it was only a prelude to the all-powerful *information age.* This is the age we are living in today. It is characterised by the digitisation and communication of information across computer networks. This power of information technology has turned the world into a global village where business firms now compete with knowledge and networking capability on a global basis. This has made the world of business become more competitive and less stable. It goes without saying that today, for one to be hired and work for a company, or for one to build his own business, requires being equipped with competitive skills. These skills are acquired through an education system.

The better the school system one enrols in, the more chances of survival they have. Without education a person is likely to live life the hard way. It is prudent for parents to be wise and provide resources for a good education for their children.

Good education is often expensive. One simple way to afford it is to have a number of children who are few enough for what your limited resources can allow. Note also that there are many parents who cannot afford taking their children to a good school, not because of the expensive tuition fees but because of the many children they have. Many parents in such situations resort to splitting their limited financial resources among the many children by enrolling them in cheap schools. However, the real cost of such a 'strategy' manifests later in time when children (who would have now grown into adults) end up graduating from school with mediocre skills. With mediocre skills, one will struggle to find a good job placement or will not have adequate skills to build a meaningful business.

As strange as it may seem, there are some parents who would bear a large number of children and hope for *chance* to one day work out its way into motivating the children to become successful in life. Now, while it is true that there are some people with legendary stories of having rose *from rags to riches*, not everyone may have the same ability, enthusiasm, skill, or favourable opportunities. Thus, it is simply foolish for a father to bear too many children whom he leaves to the chance of exceptional success stories. It is important to be aware of the fact that although we know that God holds our future, we need to play our part in making good use of the free will and intelligence He endowed us with.

Some people see planning of finances to be impractical because of the many hardships of life which wouldn't permit them to save money. Well, as long as one cherishes an excuse of being unable to do something, they will continue to hinder themselves from manifesting the potential to overcome in life. There is a story I was told of a poor couple who had opened a bank account for saving money for their children's education expenses, way before the children were born. They later invested in building houses which they put on rent. Unfortunately the couple died at the time when the children were in their secondary school. The good news is that today the children have an income for their livelihood and education which comes from the houses on rent. Clearly the parents of these children had the ability to see afar and prepare for the survival of their children. They did not take their poor condition as an excuse for failing to secure the future of their children. Wisdom, planning and investing for the future is what enabled them to achieve what they did. Such noble people ought to be emulated. (See **Appendix IV** - *Inspired by The Singapore Story*).

3. *Calculating your family's regular expenses, and comparing them against how much you earn, noting the difference and planning how to eliminate the deficit.*

Many times we find ourselves spending more money than we earn. This can many times be quite stressing. However, instead of feeling depressed at the deficits, thinking and planning on how to narrow the gap would be more helpful. This certainly is not an easy process but it is needful.

Narrowing or eliminating a budget deficit can be achieved in different ways depending on the nature of the cause of the problem. For example, there are some people whose monthly expenses are always higher than their income, not because they are poor but because of a terrible habit of always being in debt. Such are people who are so much in debt that they can't even enjoy their earned income; they have literally imprisoned themselves to work and earn for their creditors. Again, there are some couples who don't even take time to prepare a budget before they spend money; their spending is characterised by either buying whatever has attracted their eyes or what a sales-person has persuaded them to get. This reminds me of a certain friend I have who is loved by many people because of his calm personality. Unfortunately his calm and softness has become useful for every Jim and Jack who sells on the streets. One day as we were chatting he told me about how he had once bought an over-sized funny looking big trousers. *"Why did you do it?"* I asked him. He explained that he actually wasn't interested in the trousers but he had to buy it because the sales man was very insistent. Odd and funny as his explanation may sound, there are actually many people who like this good gentleman spend money to appease sales people.

It is just not wise to blow up and deplete hard-earned income. If one is like the 'good and kind' gentleman we have just mentioned, instead of suspecting a demon to be hiding in his pockets, causing money to disappear before it is used on important things, it would be wise to simply start a lifestyle of thrift spending.

A couple should always carefully plan on how they intend to spend their hard earned income. Actually, more desirable should be a plan on how money can be invested to cause it to reproduce and multiply. One method of causing money to start reproducing itself is by starting a well-planned business. Starting a business will help you build an alternative source of income. This is very important as dependence on one source of income in these hard times can be depressing. Having an additional source of income will help you be in control of your financial situation. Please note that you don't have to start with exaggerated big business ideas. Start small. Do something that you love. I remember sometime back when Norah had started a small business of selling samosas which her workmates would buy for breakfast. The money she would raise would help in meeting certain food expenses, albeit in a very small way. I was always happy to see her face brighten when she would count some cash notes and use them to buy some food stuffs. I once said to her, *"why not start making some more which I can also start selling to my work place?"* The point here is this: no matter how small an idea, it can later grow into something that can create a good *passive income* for your household. Furthermore, by creating a business parents can involve their children into its operations and thus use it as an educational tool for mentoring them in principles of managing finances and growing an investment. The family can work out a programme of reading a particular motivational book each month which can educate and motivate them on principles of growing their small business.[16] By

____

[16] You can start with *a book like IMPROVE YOUR FINANCIAL IQ* by Robert Kiyosaki. Introduce such books to your children at an early age. You and your family can also consider joining

having routine (e.g. weekly) round table discussions which are focussed on what each one has learned from a particular chapter of a book, children will be inspired to grow up into knowledgeable and successful adults.

4. *Planning for health care and insurance.*

No one loves to talk about illness, death, accidents, and other such misfortunes. However, these are things that may eventually occur to anyone of us in this troubled earthly life. It is just important to prepare for such eventualities. Without a plan for them, you will not only become a burden to other people but may actually end up getting desperate, depressed, or even destitute. With good preparation, however, bad things or disturbances that can result from misfortunes can be minimised.

There are different ways to prepare for expenses which are likely to be incurred when an undesired event occurs. Various kinds of institutions exist which provide advice and services for different facilities that can safeguard a person in times of unfortunate circumstances. Examples of facilities that have helped a lot of people include medical schemes, health insurance, life insurance, savings bank account, etc. I should emphasise that these facilities are not just important for your safety; they also prevent you from becoming desperate or a burden to other people when an unforeseen

---

educative and inspirational book clubs like the *MiTe Book Club*.

circumstance occurs. It would be wise to invest a little time to research this subject and make efforts to invest in a facility that you feel is the most important for you.

5. *Planning when you will retire.*

This is one thing most people don't do and yet it is a very crucial thing. Know that no matter how comfortable you are with your current job, one day you may have to face the reality of losing it. It is wise to imagine what would happen to you and your family if the steady income that you are currently enjoying was to suddenly stop. Yes, it is possible for your employment contract to be terminated! It doesn't have to be a dismissal; it could be a sudden health problem or even an accident that may render you unemployable. These are very unpleasant things to talk about but which are real and are affecting millions of people. Instead of avoiding talk or thoughts about the possibility of being unemployed, it would be wiser to actually start planning for it!

Whilst you are an employee of some company, it is possible to build a business which can start giving you an alternative source of income. By having such an investment, you will no longer be a slave or prisoner to your current employment contract. Apart from this you would also have secured the financial future of your children. These ideas are not just theories; they have worked for many people, especially in developed countries. To learn more about this, read Robert Kiyosaki's book,

RETIRE YOUNG, RETIRE RICH: this book has helped millions of people around the world.

IT IS IMPORTANT FOR a couple to have a number of children that they can afford to *feed, educate,* and *mentor*. The children should also be spaced in a way that will enable a couple to give full attention to an individual child before giving birth to another one. This is good for the children as well as the mother who will give herself enough time to recuperate before going through the toil of another conception.

- *Feeding*

Feeding should involve eating healthy and well balanced diets. Children who are well nourished will not only have healthy bodies but are more likely to be intelligent. Scientific research has demonstrated this fact. The impact of healthy food on intelligence appears to be more crucial especially in the first three years of a child, a period when the human brain grows very fast. Note that when these first three years of a child have been compromised with poor diet, problems that may result from that can be irreparable - *"any cognitive and behavioral effects relating to eating habits in early childhood"* notes Dr Kate Northstone, *"may well persist into later childhood, despite any subsequent changes"* (cited in Alleyne, 2011).

Clearly a husband and wife with more children than they can afford to feed are likely to provide them with food which leaves much to be desired in terms of adequacy and quality. This in turn can lead to other more serious problems such as illness, or hunger which can be making a child fail to concentrate in class at school. A couple should bear a number of children that they can afford to feed with good healthy food and well balanced meals.

- *Education*

As was earlier explained, good schools where a child can acquire quality education are often expensive. When I was young I first started my primary school in a very low-income compound. Schools in this area consisted of children coming from very poor families. Pupils used to be clustered in very large numbers in classrooms which had no desks or tables. We used to sit on the floor. The number of pupils in a class was so large that it was impossible for a teacher to give personalized attention to each learner. My performance used to be below average. Later, I was taken to stay with an aunt who lived in an area of well-to-do people. I was enrolled at a good school where classrooms had fewer pupils. The teaching was excellent, and pupils were well behaved and disciplined. The pupils also seemed to know too much. I was astounded. This experience changed my academic life: I only stayed for a year at that good school and was later transferred back to my old compound. Surprisingly, I became the best pupil in all subjects at my new school in the compound. Today when I look back I realize that I became the best pupil not because of being more intelligent than other pupils but because the other pupils had not been exposed to a quality educational environment like I had been at the good school I had transferred to.

"It's hard...there aren't many other children his age who have successfully bootstrapped a start-up."

A more important thing to note here is that many pupils coming from the good school are more likely to end up in universities and later get employed in good companies whilst only a handful from the poor school may complete their education successfully.

Now, please understand that living in a poor country like Zambia is quite a challenge; the high cost of living can many times leave a person with no option but to enroll a child in a poor school. However, it is also important to know that the little potential or opportunity one could have to afford quality education for his children gets completely squandered when one bears too many children, way beyond their financial capacity. Such a situation could make a person not to afford even a low-cost education provided by poor schools.

• *Mentorship*

Giving attention to, and mentoring, a child demands time and resources. Mentorship should impart knowledge in different areas of a child's life. Three important areas in which a child should be mentored in include his or her spiritual life, financial management skills, and general attitude (social behaviour) towards people in society.

One good method for carrying out mentorship is by introducing *mentees* to a life of reading. It would be an exciting process to choose a book to read each month. A book should be about an aspect of something you are mentoring your children in. For example you can use the book *HOW TO WIN AND INFLUENCE PEOPLE* by Dale Carnegie to inspire a child on appropriate ways to relate with different kinds of people. The children can be tasked to make notes and produce a report about lessons they have learnt or ideas they have conceived from reading a chapter. Later in the day or at the end of the week the family can hold discussions and presentations about the book. As a parent keep the discussions exciting and insightful.

Have some laughter

A young couple moved into a new neighbourhood. The next morning while eating breakfast, the young woman saw her neighbour through the window hanging the wash outside.

"*That laundry is not clean*", she said. "*She doesn't know how to wash correctly. Perhaps she needs better laundry soap.*"

Her husband looked on, but remained silent. Every time the neighbour would hang laundry to dry, the young woman would make the same comments.
About one month later, the woman was surprised to see nice clean wash on the line and she said to her husband:

"*Look, she has learnt how to wash correctly. I wonder who taught her this!*"

The husband replied:

"*I got up early this morning and cleaned our windows.*"

5.
Raising Children

"In the world's broad field of battle, in the bivouac of Life, Be not like dumb, driven cattle. Be the hero in the strife!"

Longfellow's Poem

"Train up a child in the way he should go: and when he is old, he will not depart from it. The rich ruleth over the poor, and the borrower is servant to the lender"

Psalm 22:6-7

Because of cute chubby cheeks?

We were chatting with a friend (who is financially struggling to raise his two children) when he said:

"I am thinking of having three more children!"

"Why?" I asked him.

"Well, you know toddlers look so cute with their chubby cheeks", he explained. I could not help but caution him:

"It takes a moment to make a baby, but a lifetime to raise it! Those cute chubby cheeks are not of a doll but a human being who soon grows into an adult to face the challenges of this world."

Having children is not wrong, but if one lives on the same planet I do, he or she knows that this is a troublesome world which requires sufficient resources and time to raise and equip a child for a better and meaningful life. Unfortunately, it seems many parents are unaware of the *real* cost of raising children. "Cost" *here* does not just refer to the price of food or school tuition fees for the children; as will be discussed shortly, there is so much more that goes with parenting than that. If a father and mother haven't done their homework, they will keep bearing children of which they won't have the time and resources to provide mentorship. And without mentorship children grow up without direction, trying out things their own way. Although some succeed through this hard way, many are left behind being tossed around by the world like trash, growing up as sad disgruntled adults. If you are a parent and are reading this, please never do such an injustice to your children; they never wrote an application letter asking to come into this world; their failure or success is your responsibility!

I should emphasise that to effectively raise children requires mentorship. Mentorship involves friendship and a heart-to-heart communication between a *mentor* and a *mentee*. Furthermore, effective mentorship requires a mentee to have faith in the mentor. This faith may naturally occur if the mentor has the experience of things he is trying to impart into his student. Unfortunately, many parents are nowhere close to being role models to their children as their lives have little to demonstrate in terms of character, focus, and virtue. If you are a parent in such a situation but are now determined to change, the following framework of five principles can be a good start.

Five principles

Parents should teach their children the following five principles:

The principle of:

- having *foresight* and *managing* time
- having *focus* and *discipline*
- being in control of money
- love, and
- self-respect

1. *The principle of having foresight and managing time*

How a person lives his daily life tells about how they view time. Some people live their lives as though time is like a *circle* and others like it is a *line*. The person who treats time like a circle may regard the 11:30 AM of today to be the same one for tomorrow.

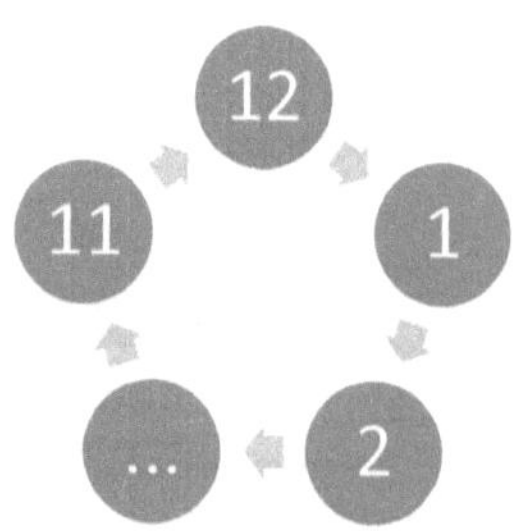

Viewing time like a circle

So, if he feels lazy to perform a task today at 11:30 AM, he may not feel much bothered as there will be another 11:30 AM tomorrow. On the other hand, a person who sees time like a line knows that the time lost today can never be recovered and hence the need to manage it properly and avoid procrastinations. However, the urge to manage time properly cannot start suddenly in a person. It can only occur in a person who is looking forward to achieving something at a certain point in time.

Viewing time linearly

The continuous desire to reach a desired goal is what produces the character of avoiding time-wasting activities. A person with such a character regards each new day as another opportunity to achieve their potentials. Like a driver who doesn't want to waste fuel by aimless driving or idling of the engine, he or she avoids living through a day chatting or passing time without doing valuable activities.

A person who doesn't value time and planning usually lives below their God-given potentials. Such a person often lacks passion for anything and hence is full of procrastinations. It is only a matter of time when such a person will one day realise that his or her muscles have stiffened, failing to do simple tasks that they once could do easily. Old age would have caught up with them.

2. *Principle of having focus and discipline*

I was once told a parable about why a lion, and not a hyena, is a king of the jungle. A lion despite being not the strongest or the biggest animal in the jungle happens to have precision and focus when it wants to hunt prey. When it sees a herd of impalas; no matter how many good looking ones will be there, it will only aim for one. A hyena on the other hand, the story goes, lacks focus. It will see one impala, begin chasing it, and then later shift its attention to a more attractive one. At the end of the hunt poor hyena catches nothing and only ends up eating carcasses left by other animals.

In many families there are 'hyenas' who could have been in a position of leadership and inspiration but the lack of focus and discipline made them end up living off other people's resources. Some families have pitiful cases of persons growing up into adults but who are still living under their parents' shelter, ever requesting for assistance.

Take note that focus and discipline build on the preceding principle of having a goal. It is a goal that makes a person focus his energy and resources. Hence no matter how talented or financially-able a person can be, if they lack focus and discipline, they will always be at loss of various ventures that lure attention. Children must be nurtured from a young age to avoid living aimlessly and haphazardly. When children become trained to view and treat time linearly (i.e. like a straight line) it will make them aware that time is a fleeting resource. People who view time as a fleeting resource become alert to the fact that one day they will exit this world either through old age, sickness, an accident or some other circumstance. This awareness inspires a sense of urgency in them, making them become conscientious in the way they spend their time and resources in trying to accomplish set objectives.

A child should be encouraged to be focussed on the kind of future he desires and then work towards  achieving that goal. He should be warned against living an aimless life which lacks the passion of purpose or direction. A good parent will take keen interest in a child's career or other goals, and do the best to provide the moral, emotional and material support.

In all this, however, let the child be raised in a manner of always being conscious of the blessing of prayerfully seeking God's will over his desires. Let the child be taught that *"ye ought to say, If the Lord will, we shall live, and do this, or that"* (James 4:15).

Let the child know that God, our Father, is a great planner and He desires the same of His children and that is why He gave them intelligence: yes, God has given as intelligence to plan and do things wisely, even as we wait upon His will: for *"to man belong the plans of the heart"* says the

Scripture, *"but from the LORD comes the reply of the tongue. All man's ways seem innocent to him, but motives are weighed by the LORD. Commit to the LORD whatever you do, and your plans will succeed"* (Proverbs 16:1-3, NIV). In another place again the Scripture admonishes to *"delight thyself also in the LORD; and he shall give thee the desires of thine heart. Commit thy way unto the LORD; trust also in him; and he shall bring it to pass"* (Psalm 37:4).

3.   *Principle of being in control of money*

Some believers take faith to mean having no regard for the future but only getting concerned with what is happening in the present. There is a verse often used for justifying this attitude: it is about when the Lord said to his disciples not to carry food or money on their journey; He *"commanded them that they should take nothing for their journey, save a staff only; no scrip, no bread, no money in their purse"* for *"the morrow shall take thought for the things of itself. Sufficient unto the day is the evil thereof"* (Mark 6:8, Matthew 6:31, 34). One wonders whether believers with such an attitude have also read where the Lord later admonished the disciples saying: *"And he said unto them, When I sent you without purse, and scrip, and shoes, lacked ye any thing? And they said, Nothing. Then said he unto them, But now, he that hath a purse, let him take it, and likewise his scrip: and he that hath no sword, let him sell his garment, and buy one"* (Luke 22:35-36).

Some believers shun any form of discussion about the subject of money because of the gross damage done to the subject by charismatic prosperity preachers. These preachers have brought a great reproach on the Gospel as they have literally made merchandise out of congregants just as was foretold by saint Peter:

> *But there were false prophets also among the people, even as there shall be false teachers among you...And many shall follow their pernicious ways; by reason of whom the way of truth shall be evil spoken of. And through covetousness shall they with feigned words make merchandise of you* (2 Peter 2:1-3).

This Scripture has fulfilled today as there is widespread carnality in churches. Long gone are the days when a sinner entered a church and found himself in tears of repentance; now sinners go to church only to get armed with business acumen. This is quite unfortunate. Nevertheless, it should not hinder true believers from approaching the subject in a sober way.

Norah and I have never had ambitions of becoming rich. However, we have committed ourselves to always work towards putting money under our control so that it doesn't end up controlling us. Notice that money can either rule over a person or they can rule over it.

Let us look at these concepts in a little more detail.

- *A person controlled by money*

Money rules over a person when his or her state of peace is dictated by money; its absence can lead to their high blood pressure, stress, frustration, or moods. Being in the state of lack in turn causes a person to become a burden to other people, as they will often be in a situation of requesting for financial and other forms of assistance from them. Such a person lives at the mercy of other people and hence loses self-respect. When sickness falls upon such a destitute or his family, they will not be able to afford proper health care facilities. This condition of poverty can lead to untimely deaths in the family. Now, blow this illustration to a large scale and you will understand why the UN data on life-spans of populations in different countries has most of the poor countries of the world (many from Africa) at the bottom of the list.

The problem of poverty in Africa and other Third World regions of the world have mainly been blamed on mediocre political leadership. One prominent economist (Moyo,2009) has presented this case well. However, it is also important to recognise the fact that the culture of ignorance, lack of planning and focus at family-unit levels has been a great contributor to the problem. In this cruel and indifferent world, children have to be taught that the world owes them nothing! They need to learn that they are in the great race of time which offers many woes just as it offers opportunities; if they happen to fall at a point in this race, they can either blame another person, a stone in the way, or whatever circumstance, and stay down as they cry at their loss. However, the truth of the matter is that what makes a loser in the race is not the *falling down* but the *staying down*.

<table>
<tr><td colspan="2" align="center">A person controlled by money</td></tr>
<tr><td align="center">$</td><td>He or she is most likely to be:

•   *a burden to other people*
•   *unhealthy*
•   *failing to take care of own medical expenses*
•   *sad*
•   *moody*
•   *melancholy*</td></tr>
</table>

Children need to be taught about how money operates (regardless of how little it is): how to earn, save, or invest it. They have to be taught a lifestyle of being thrift. When they become adults and get employed, they have to be taught that a salary they receive is like a seed of grain – it can either be eaten, kept, or replanted in the field. If replanted it will yield more seed to provide a sustainable future. That word "*sustainable*" is important. It refers to a state of being able to continue for a long time. For example, if you have a poor neighbour who always comes to your house to ask for fish for his dinner, and you always give him out of your kindness, the solution you are providing for the man, however benevolent it seems, is not a good one; it is short term – he will eat and come back again and again. A better solution in this simplistic illustration would be to teach him how to fish; that way he will survive longer even in the event of you shifting away from the area, leaving him alone. Teaching him to fish would be a sustainable solution because it will yield results that will continue to sustain him for a long time.

From the illustration in the foregoing, we should be able to see why many poor families often remain poor; it is often a result of a parent's lack of focus to invest into something which his children can later build on. So, the children start building their lives from scratch. If they are also ignorant and visionless, the vicious cycle continues. Children of visionary parents on the other hand begin their lives from the investments that their parents left for them. As in the words of Scripture, *"A good man leaveth an inheritance to his children's children"* (Proverbs 13:22). If the children had been properly mentored, they will accumulate the wealth in a responsible manner and also leave it for their children. This continues with successive generations and it becomes a *virtuous cycle*!

I believe that a Christian can keep a sober balance of learning about how to manage money without being enticed into its lure; the objective of a child of God should be to have money under their control so that it doesn't dictate their sense of peace. I do not believe that a life of being ever in stress and being a burden to others ever glorifies

God. The following verses of scripture seem to strike a chord with this sentiment:

- *"I have been young, and now am old; yet have I not seen the righteous forsaken, nor his seed begging bread"* (Psalm 37:25).

- *"Neither did we eat any man's bread for nought; but wrought with labour and travail night and day, that we might not be chargeable to any of you...For even when we were with you, this we commanded you, that if any would not work, neither should he eat. For we hear that there are some which walk among you disorderly, working not at all, but are busybodies. Now them that are such we command and exhort by our Lord Jesus Christ, that with quietness they work, and eat their own bread"* (2 Thessalonians 3:8-12).

- *"Through wisdom is an house builded; and by understanding it is established: And by knowledge shall the chambers be filled with all precious and pleasant riches"* (Proverbs 24:3).

What we see in the above scriptures is the need for knowledge and wisdom in the managing of one's financial life. Unfortunately many people have resorted to *casting out* "demons of poverty" or praying and fasting for miracle blessings, and all such acts of fanaticism. Much as such acts can be done sincerely, we should be aware that it is possible to be sincerely wrong. One thing is certain; God has made this world to operate on certain laws for which no amount of emotionalism can alter. Consider this: a seed grows when it has been planted in the ground; a man who lays it on the table in his living room hoping for some miracle to occur for it to grow and produce roots and leaves is surely acting crazy. Much as God is able to do miracles, He is not a magician who performs His works of wonder just to amuse people's curiosity. God performs a miracle when it is really necessary for Him to do so in order to achieve a certain purpose.

The need for a man to take responsibility for his future and livelihood of his wife and children can never be over-emphasised.

- *A person in control of money*

A person who is in control of money is one who has developed the skill of managing it and is therefore not a slave of *wants* which one fails to satisfy because of the lack of resources. Like the Psalmist he can confidently say, *"The Lord is my shepherd; I shall not want"* (Psalm 23:1).

A person who has money under his control is not influenced by its temptation. This means that being rich doesn't necessary mean that one is in control of money because there are people who are rich and whose God is money – it controls their minds and behaviour; it leads them into promiscuity, pride, and gluttony. Because of wealth they lose their true identity as mortal beings. Such are not free people but slaves to earthly possessions. However, a person in control of money is not lured by its presence; he or she instead honours the Lord with his *substance* and with the *firstfruits* of his increase – "*Honour the Lord with thy substance*" admonishes the Scripture, "*and with the firstfruits of all thine increase: so shall thy barns be filled with plenty*" (Proverbs 3:9-10).

A person who has gained control over finances is independent and is even able to help people in need. Being free from the stress of lack, he or she will be healthier and cheerful.

A person in control of money

	He or she is most likely to be: • *a giver* • *not a burden to other people* • *able to manage own medical expenses.* • *independent* • *healthy* • *cheerful*
$	

Please note that this book is not about *how* to be in control of money. For this subject I would strongly recommend two books by Robert T. Kiyosaki: "*RICH DAD, POOR DAD: What The Rich Teach Their Kids About Money That The Poor And Middle Class Do Not*" and "*INCREASE YOUR FINANCIAL IQ: Get Smarter With Your Money.*"

4. *The principle of love*

This four-letter word is the theme of most songs, movies, and a lot of social media conversations but yet is the least understood. Any person who falls for its misconception stands at the blink of ruining his or her life. There are many young ladies who once had a fine life and prospects of a bright future but not until they got married to an abusive husband. Likewise there are many young men who were once happy but have ended up living a depressed life after marrying a woman who happens to be a female but just nothing close to what can be called a "sweetheart" – a humble and lovely woman.

The danger of a son or daughter being found in a troublesome marriage can be avoided if parents invest time in mentoring their son or daughter. Through mentorship a bond of friendship between parents and children will form. That bond is a social glue that should be characterised by virtues of:

- appreciating one another.

- showing concern, kindness and empathy for each other's situations.

- kind and respectful language.

- being fond of each other's company.

- reading and discussing books and current events together as a family.

If such a relationship between children and parents exists, children will see in their parents mentors, role models, and an inspiration. Such an association with children imparts virtues on them which will make children uncomfortable with company that is disrespectful. A young man or woman who grows up in a loving environment becomes loving and has more chances of ending up in a relationship with a respectable decent person who has similar virtues. As the old proverb states, birds of same feathers flock together.

5. *The principle of self-respect*

A parent may sometimes admire children of other parents because of the excellent demeanour and sense of humility and respect they exhibit. There are some parents who would even wish they had such children. Such children would be mindful about what to speak to someone and how he or she may feel about their words. Many times such youths tend to be likeable by everyone, and sometimes favour seems to naturally follow them. It may all seem like they are just gifted with virtue. However, such character has more to do with a kind of home environment a child was raised in; an abusive environment breeds abusive children and likewise a virtuous family environment produces virtuous children.

APART FROM ALL THAT has been said it is important to be aware that we live in an evil wicked world, full of demonic influences. It is important that you always pray for your family for God's grace and protection because *"we wrestle not against flesh and blood, but against principalities, against powers, against the rulers of the darkness of this world, against spiritual wickedness in high places"* (Ephesians 6:12). We live in a world where moral perversion has reached its zenith as strange immoral concepts camouflaged in the name of human rights have found their way in colleges, universities, and work places. If you are not close enough with your children to mentor them and develop a strong bond of friendship with them, the devil will surely exploit the opportunity. It is just important that regardless of how busy you are, always know that your children should be your first full-time 'work' before anything else. If your job completely robs you of time with them, think twice about what you can do about the situation.

Have some laughter

On the first night of their honeymoon, the husband isn't sure how to tell his bride about his stinky feet and smelly socks, while the wife is wondering how to break the news to him about her awful breath, which so far, she's been able to cover up.

After some soul-searching, the husband gathers his nerve and says,
"I have a confession."

She draws closer, peers into his eyes, and says,
"Darling, so do I."

Recoiling, he says,
"Don't tell me—you've eaten my socks"

6.
FOR WOMEN
Ten things a woman should know

Notes *by* Norah Phiri

Used to counsel women who are about to marry or wives going through marital problems.

(Reproduced in this book by permission)

"Look your best and be your best...you ought to be as sweet and fresh and everything as you can be when your husband comes...you ought to meet him at the door...with just a kiss as sweet to him as it was the day you kissed him at the altar to be your husband"

William Branham

"Who can find a virtuous woman? for her price is far above rubies. The heart of her husband doth safely trust in her...Strength and honour are her clothing...She openeth her mouth with wisdom; and in her tongue is the law of kindness...She looketh well to the ways of her household, and eateth not the bread of idleness...Her children arise up, and call her blessed; her husband also, and he praiseth her"

Proverbs 31:10-28

Marriage is beautiful!

I have been blessed with a wonderful marriage. I have no regrets. This is not because my husband and I are perfect; it is simply a result of the coming together of two imperfect persons who are willing and patient enough to be perfected by God. The more we look into God's Word as the standard of our perfection, the better and more enjoyable our journey of love has become. Contrary to what we kept hearing from people (prior to our marriage), that the longer a couple stays together the lesser their affection grows, ours has been a different experience altogether: with time our love, attachment and maturity seems to keep strengthening. Although we acknowledge this to have been the work of God's grace, we trust that even when it is grace, it takes responsible and cautious hands to handle the grace. This involves deliberately adopting a kind of lifestyle that should prove one to be worthy of the grace that God has given him or her. This may involve adhering to certain wise principles.

Dear fellow woman, kindly permit me to share some ten insights that I have found useful in experiencing the joy of marriage.

1. Respect

In the book of Proverbs we read that "*Every wise woman buildeth her house: but the foolish plucketh it down with her hands*" (14:1). If you want to destroy your marriage, begin with disrespecting your husband.   Have you ever come across women who are just so loud and bossy? As a woman you cannot honour God and be disrespectful to your husband. In the Bible we have an example of Sarah; she called her husband *"Lord"*. Furthermore, we are admonished to respect and submit unto our own husbands, as unto the Lord (Ephesians 5:22).

Disrespect to a husband is often manifested in so many ways. A simple example is a woman who talks while her husband is also talking over a misunderstanding they have had.   Prudence requires that a wife humbly and quietly listens to the husband as he tries to address a misunderstanding which has occurred; a prudent wife ought to observe this no matter how unhappy she may be about a situation. As women there is a way of expressing our view or concern in a humble and respectful way. Let us be aware of our husband's presence and his position of headship over us. This in no way means suppressing our rights. Actually, a woman who treats her husband as her king, makes him to treat her as his queen. And on the other hand a woman who is so proud that she feels submission is being old fashioned is on her way of experiencing what God's Word speaks regarding such an attitude – *"when pride cometh, then cometh shame: but with the lowly is wisdom"* (Proverbs 11:2).

Never belittle your husband, by doing so you are actually injuring him. We have many times heard stories of how a well-to-do man decided to leave a comfortable life which he once had with a gorgeous career woman, for a quite charming girl who happened to give him attention and respect. Of course that would be a wrong thing for a Christian man to do because one problem (or sin) cannot *atone* for another one. However, we ought to be aware that if a believer is careless, she can open doors of temptation to a man. Such temptations could many times be avoided if a woman performs her roles as a wife in a man's life. One such role is sex.

2. Sex

Sex is one important way for a couple to express their love. Sex in marriage plays a very big role; it brings spouses close together.

As women we need to enjoy sex with our husbands; you should never take sex with your husband as an inconvenience; instead, always show your husband that you are available for him anytime (except in moments of sickness, menstruation, or consecration to prayer and fasting – 1 Corinthians 7:5) . Please understand that a woman is different from a man. A man needs sex more often than a woman. This is a physiological difference. It is natural. Some men may need sex three or four times in a week whilst women only once after a considerable period of time. So, in understanding this difference, a wife should not starve her husband.

Apart from bonding each other, sexual intimacy can relieve your husband of stress. I have seen it in my husband; He sometimes gets stressed with various challenges that need to be overcome. However, I love to see the sight of his face when we expressed our love: he looks satisfied, happy, and ready to conquer the world for me and our children.

One important mistake couples make is to let their sex life become a boring routine. Dear lady, please understand that it is your responsibility to keep the sex life of your marriage exciting. Be romantic to him. Stop dressing like you are about to do some garden work when you are actually in the bedroom. That's your bedroom; it has a door and key for a purpose. The purpose should work to the fullest! In that room you can make yourself look attractive to your husband. He is all yours and you are his and so there is no reason to be ashamed. Buy some 'bedroom-only' kind of clothing that will arouse his appetite for you! When he looks at you let words of the Song of Solomon come to his mind – *"Thy navel is like a round goblet, which wanteth not liquor: thy belly is like an heap of wheat set about with lilies. Thy two breasts are like two young roes that are twins"* (Song of Solomon 7:1).

During sex, try to be creative and make your husband feel excited. Have a fore-play before sex during which you can talk, play and cuddle each other. Yes, you can even dance for him! Let your husband admire you as you slowly take off your clothes and begin to embrace. Make every moment memorable for your husband. Make him to be coming for more and more of you. Be informed that sexual satisfaction also helps to keep your man's eyes away from temptations!

Now there are some women who have a tendency of denying their husbands sex when they are upset. This is being immature and it is not right. Never let a misunderstanding interfere with your love-life. A misunderstanding should be treated as a misunderstanding and love as another thing altogether.

3. Don't compare your husband to other men in trying to change him

It is not wise to compare your husband, who is trying his best to work hard for you, to other men in terms of their success, looks, or achievements. Other wives would even go to extents of complaining about things that their daddy used to do for them which their husbands are failing to do.

It is important to appreciate the fact that every human being is unique. You need to accept the man you married the way he is. Here we are not talking about letting him to continue wearing checked trousers with striped shirts. But, something on this line: if you came from a well-to-do family with a certain status and your husband from a middle or low-income home, do not force him to start putting on appearances to suit your status. The joy of marriage can never be found in the keeping up of appearances. Unfortunately, there are many couples who live above their means, drive expensive vehicles and rent above-average homes, all this being done in an effort to impress on-lookers. Some couples put on such expensive outlooks but whilst being eaten alive by huge loans they have accumulated for their fictitious lifestyle. It is simply vanity to put on looks to appease people who don't even bother about your status. Instead of trying to influence your husband to live a lifestyle of some rich neighbour you envy, be happy with him and tell him that he is the best thing that happened to you and that you are proud of his efforts to make his family happy.

Now, ofcourse there are certain situations where a man is a busybody, lazing around and never wanting to work. That would be an unfortunate situation as it will put the family in problems. Commit the situation in prayer, and if you want to talk to your husband, do it with respect and try to communicate with his heart instead of throwing tantrum which may provoke his anger.

Now, another wrong thing women like to do is to discourage their husbands from something they love to do. A wife may have a dislike for something which the husband enjoys to do. It is funny how such a simple thing can produce tension between spouses. *"He only spends time reading books and doesn't give me any attention!"* some women complain. Well, marriage is about two people with different backgrounds and lifestyles coming together to be fused into one. So, rather than despising or discouraging your spouse from a certain activity or hobby that you don't like, it would be more helpful for you to join him in that activity and enjoy the life together. Ofcourse this can only apply to certain activities. For example, Andrew is a 'bookworm', and he loves to write; he can be on books and on the laptop from 6 Am to 6 PM! Intermittently he will move away from the desk and come to explain to me something that has excited him and the only thing I would hear is some language from Mars. I can tell he has really enjoyed the point he was reading but I just can't understand the stuff about *cosmology, quantum mechanics,* etcetera. Well, he has made me join a Book Club where members vote on a book to read for the month after which they will meet to share insights learned. I didn't know reading could be so informative and much fun at the same time! Within a short time I have felt becoming more knowledgeable on a lot of things. So, from this I learned that instead of trying to change your husband about a certain activity or hobby he loves, try to take part. This attitude will not only add knowledge to your worldview but will strengthen your social-glue with your hubby. Every human being enjoys company which shares a common interest and so this will even be most appropriate with your best friend – your husband!

4. Beware of being a career woman who gets too busy to serve her husband

As the world gets busier and the cost of living going up, more than ever before women are now finding themselves in employment to supplement their husband's efforts. This is alright considering the hard times we are living in. I am also working. However, this situation has made some women become too busy or too tired to give attention to their husbands. Other women have so completely lost their womanhood that they have to hire maids to do everything in the house; from cooking and serving of the husband's food to the cleaning of their matrimonial bedroom. The routine of such women is to get up early in the morning and rush to the office, attend to business, get tired, return home, and relax in the sofa whilst watching TV as the maids fix supper. Such a woman is more married and committed to her business than the husband. What is more, she hardly has any time to mentor the children together with her husband. This just doesn't seem right according to the standards of God's Word. Could the current situation of our society having many young boys and girls who seem to lack simple decency in terms of their manner of dressing, behaviour, and attitudes, be the result of this new trend where husbands and wives are both too busy for family life?

No matter how tired you are as a wife, take time to serve your husband; ensure his cloths are washed and ironed properly. Remember that your husband is your number one duty and any other thing should come second. Ensure his stomach is full with good food. There are some husbands who get to their offices feeling hungry and have to eat breakfast prepared by some secretary or one bought from some *fast-food* shop. Just what happened to the old tradition of a wife ensuring that her husband has eaten a well prepared and healthy breakfast? I am afraid that modern women are losing values that once defined a woman at an alarming rate. My husband often asks: could the reason behind the current high divorce-rates be that most men are now marrying human beings who happen to be physically female but are actually men in their lifestyles? Lord have mercy.

5. Dress modestly

As women, let us do all things to glorify God. This should include the manner of our dressing. God's Word admonishes us to dress modestly – *"in like manner also, that women adorn themselves in modest apparel, with shamefacedness and sobriety"* (1 Timothy 2:9). As my husband often says, if God is only concerned about what is in our hearts and not what we dress, this scripture would not have been in the Bible. Elsewhere we are also told that when God called Jacob and his family, they were required to change their clothing (Genesis 35:2). And the Lord Jesus Christ warned that *"whosoever looketh on a woman to lust after her hath committed adultery with her already in his heart"* (Matthew 5:28). What can these words mean but that our dressing can cause men to lust after us and therefore the need for us to mind the way we dress? Many times we have heard about how some husbands sinned with a secretary at his office or some other woman. Do not such illicit relationships often begin with the lusting after a woman's body? Clearly, this temptation to the man is worsened when a woman exposes her legs or breasts, through wearing of skimpy, short or *see-*

through outfits. No matter how such a woman can claim to be a decent person, according to God's Word she is immoral and causing men to sin.

It is so sad today to see how there is no longer a difference in the dressing styles of people of the world and many Christians. More unfortunate is how even elderly women have also been caught up in the frenzy of fashion. One wonders who is now there to advise the younger girls. What has happened is that wrong things have been repeated over and over again and have become so widespread until they appear to be right and the right things seem to be odd and wrong. But if we are Christians we are not supposed to be tossed about with the blowing winds of change - *"stand ye in the ways, and see, and ask for the old paths, where is the good way, and walk therein, and ye shall find rest for your souls"* (Jeremiah 6:16).

6. Keep a distance from other men

It is not right and not wise for a married woman to have a male friend, whether at the work place or anywhere else. Just as you would not be comfortable seeing your husband always on long chats with a female friend so it is also not right for you to be involved in such kinds of communication. Communication is very powerful; it can begin a relationship with someone which you never imagined could start. Do not trust yourself too much; the Bible says that *"the heart is deceitful above all things, and desperately wicked: who can know it?"* (Jeremiah 17:9). Beware, communication with a male can start so innocent and formal. Slowly you will begin getting close and too comfortable with the person until your heart starts getting attached to him. Many have gone through that path only to end up destroying a precious marriage they once had with their spouse.

How you relate with people and carry yourself as a married woman is important. If you are in regular employment and often find yourself in environments where there are males, you ought to carry yourself with self-respect and set boundaries which should easily be discerned by people. Men will treat you according to the way you carry yourself. Being a jovial kind of a woman who always wants to participate in any kind of talk and laughter is just simply not befitting a virtuous woman!

7. Be always clean and neat

Apart from the purpose of hygiene, cleanliness is important for your man. No man is happy to arrive home finding a wife who is looking untidy with uncombed hair, smelling sweat, and in a kitchen full of dirty dishes, with various things scattered around. *"Look your best and be your best...you ought to be as sweet and fresh and everything as you can be when your husband comes...you ought to meet him at the door...with just a kiss as sweet to him as it was the day you kissed him at the altar to be your husband"*, admonished brother Branham (1957).

Being a dirty woman is awful. A woman and her house should be clean. A home is the one place where a woman's imagination has to be expressed in terms of colours, cleanliness, and beauty in general. It is one place a woman should feel good about herself.

Some women leave all the house work to be performed by the maid without any of their participation whatsoever. As the maid is performing the house chores, the woman is sunk in a sofa, watching all the channels on TV. Get involved in your home to supervise the young girls or maids, ensuring that they do perfect work. If you are always busy with office work, don't let that rob your natural status of being a woman. You were born as a woman and not whatever title this world has given you. And remember that no matter how you succeed anywhere else in the world, your glory as a woman is in the man and in raising your children (1 Corinthians 11:7, 1 Timothy 2:15). So, as Andrew often puts it in the *Believers Couples Fellowship* meetings, a failure in life is not that woman who is selling tomatoes on the road side, but the rich and career lady who fails to be a good wife.

8. Prayer

The Bible tells us to pray without ceasing, because the evil one is always looking for whom to devour. It is not good to take things for granted just because your husband is a Christian, anointed, or prayerful. If you have been blessed with a husband who values and adores you, you should even have more reason to be more prayerful as the adversary certainly doesn't like the joy of marriage. You ought to pray for your husband and family for God's protection and blessings. Pray for your husband to be successful in what he does; that the Lord may bless the work of his hands. When things are not okay and there is no food at home, instead of adding to the stress of the man by complaining, hold him by his hand and tell him, *"honey, don't worry; you have always worked hard to keep us safe, and I trust God will reward your efforts; let us commit the situation in God's hands."* A husband will certainly be encouraged and will enjoy the company of such a woman. God will also bless such a unity and love.

As a woman, let your prayer also extend to your children. Bear in mind that they live in a time which is so evil. Their young minds are exposed to so many wrong things in their school environment, among their peers, through social media and the internet. This makes prayer all the more important now.

9. Discipline

Some women are all over and everywhere. Name any party in the neighbourhood and they will be there. This could be a kitchen party, a wedding, or just some other activity. While there is nothing wrong with attending functions, it does not mean that we need to attend every one of them. If you are always a busy 'bee' with such activities what time will you have with your husband, family or children? It is important as a woman to use some of your free time to be alone to yourself to improve your cooking skills, remodel the looks of your home, or read a book on health, spiritual growth or personal development. You should also make time to do bodily exercises to keep healthy and maintain a good body shape. This is important: some women are just careless both with the way they eat and the way they look. With time their stomachs bulge out as other body parts go out of shape. I don't think a husband would be happy with looking at a shapeless darling. This is something you can control by living a disciplined life of healthy eating combined with regular exercises.

Discipline is important to help us keep a balance in life. Discipline involves keeping away from activities which may be exciting but may just end up robbing us of the precious time we can use for other more worthwhile things.

10. Company and association

We become like those whom we associate with. Show me your friends, and it won't be difficult to tell what kind of a person you really are. As a Christian married woman, what kind of friends do you have? If you associate with women who always gossip about people, you also will become used to such a bad lifestyle.

Many women are so careless in discussing their marital problems with other people. Usually such behaviour shows the lack of oneness or closeness one has with her husband. A couple who are truly and completely united with each other are best of friends and cannot slander against each other. Your husband should be your pride, and it just doesn't make sense for you to talk ill about him. What you may not realise is that the same people you gossip with about your husband may amplify the story and pass it on to other gossipers who are in their other circles. A virtuous woman speaks good of her husband, even when she knows of his certain shortcomings. It is important to know that marriage involves two imperfect people coming together to be perfected by God.

IN CONCLUSION, LET THE woman of Proverbs 31:10-28 be our aspiration: *"Who can find a virtuous woman? for her price is far above rubies. The heart of her husband doth safely trust in her...Strength and honour are her clothing...She openeth her mouth with wisdom; and in her tongue is the law of kindness...She looketh well to the ways of her household, and eateth not the bread of idleness...Her children arise up, and call her blessed; her husband also, and he praiseth her."*

Have some laughter

A therapist has a theory that couples who make love once a day are the happiest. So he tests it at a seminar by asking those assembled,

"How many people here make love once a day?"

Half the people raise their hands, each of them grinning widely.

"Once a week?" A third of the audience members raise their hands, their grins a bit less vibrant.

"Once a month?" A few hands tepidly go up.

Then he asks, *"OK, how about once a year?"*
One man in the back jumps up and down, jubilantly waving his hands. The therapist is shocked—this disproves his theory.

"If you make love only once a year," he asks, *"why are you so happy?"*

The man yells, *"Today's the day!"*

Questions & Answers

1. *"I love my wife but I get attracted to a certain beautiful woman at my work place. What is making matters worse is that she also seems to be interested in me because I have observed her intimate advances towards me. I have to be frank that I am really getting attracted to her. Her looks are so appealing. I have prayed for God to deliver me out of this sin but each time I happen to start chatting with her, it suddenly seems so innocent for me to love her. What can I do?"*

When I was in primary school I remember learning about how the North Pole of a magnet repels another North Pole and a North Pole attracts with a South Pole. Later, in secondary school we learnt that things are composed of tiny particles which consists of negative and positive charges; like-charges repel and opposite charges attract and the only way to stop or weaken the attraction is to keep a distance between the unlike charges. Growing up a little older in life, I came to know that when a male begins to get closer to a female, a romantic attraction ignites. And, it goes without saying that just like poles of a magnet or charges of particles, in order to avoid the attraction and resulting inappropriate relationship, a male should keep a distance from a female, otherwise lust, a *pull* that will ultimately lead into fornication, will begin to develop. You cannot get rid of that pull by prayer and fasting against some imagined demon-power. A male who is always in close company with a female, believing that he is spiritual enough to overcome the temptation of lust, is not more deceived than a stone that would suspend in the air hoping to defy the pull of gravity.

We have a Biblical example of a man who was wise and acted right about this matter - Joseph; he did not stay around that seductive woman to try to convert her; he fled! However, this is not just a matter of fleeing; if you are sincere enough and you truly serve God with your spirit, you will not only keep away from any appearance of evil but you will rebuke, in no uncertain terms, any opposite sex who makes intimate advances towards you. Much as the devil influences people into promiscuity, he never forces anyone into such filth; the power to choose and reject temptation is in your hands. The problem is that you could be saying *"I don't want to sin"* and yet your heart desires to partake of the sin. You may wonder, *"But, I have been praying against this temptation and that shows that I don't desire sin!"* Not exactly so. There are many times that people speak prayers which are void of sincerity. Your prayer about this inappropriate relationship is one such example: you are praying for God to deliver you from this situation but yet are entertaining the woman's seductive advances towards you. Please *"be not deceived; God is not mocked: for whatsoever a man soweth, that shall he also reap"* (Galatians 6:7). Any man who is serious about being faithful to his wife will rebuke a seductive woman who tries to flirt with him. A seductive woman can only make intimate advances towards a man if he tolerates her.

So, sir, your question of **"what can I do?"** lacks sincerity; get right with God and confess your sin to him. What you are doing is wrong; you are bringing trouble on your innocent wife and that is wickedness. From what you have written, I see a backslider who is not close to God; a backslider who probably usually feeds his mind with wrong immoral stuff. To overcome sin you have to submit to God, walking in fellowship with Him. A man who dwells in the presence of God hates the smell of sin. Sin becomes an offensive smell. When such a person rejects the devil, that wicked spirit won't linger around to entertain him. Apostle James admonishes us in his epistle: *"Submit yourselves therefore to God. Resist the devil, and he will flee from you"* (James 4:7). Resisting the devil does not mean shouting prayers into the air: the temptation is not occurring in the air but in your mind. And the mind is fed by what ears hear and what eyes see. If a believer becomes lukewarm, and does not have a daily devotion of prayer and listening to messages that will nourish his spirit, he or she becomes vulnerable to evil spirits which are around the different places he may visit. Your mind requires protection by continually yielding it to God in prayer and hearing His Word – *"And be not* *conformed to this world: but be ye transformed by the renewing of your mind, that ye may prove what is that good, and acceptable, and perfect, will of God"* (Romans 12:2).

2. **"We have been taught that it is a sin to practise family planning, especially using methods of condoms or contraceptive pills. So, with my wife we've tried to use the natural method but which is not working well for us. We now have three children and are expecting our fourth. We sometimes get tempted to start using condoms but then we read Genesis 38:8-9 and are reminded that children come from God and it is sinful to waste them in a condom."**

This is sad. When a person believes wrong he or she also lives wrong. Unfortunately, if it is a couple that believes wrong, it is children who will suffer for the wrong beliefs.

There is nothing wrong for a couple to plan when they would like to have children, or how many of them they intend to have. We are not living in the ancient days of Jacob when a couple could have as many as twelve children. Today such a large family would be too large for a parent to sustain and mentor. For example, are you going to afford the cost of good quality education for all the children? There are some people who would retort by claiming that believers ought to live by faith and trust God for the provision of food and finances. Yes, God takes care of people of faith, but it is also important to know that He doesn't take care of carelessness. God has endowed human beings with something that differentiates them from animals; it is called *free will.* The *OXFORD ADVANCED LEARNERS DICTIONARY* defines free will as *"the power to make your own decisions without being controlled by God or fate."* The producing of children by a husband and wife is one example of an activity which involves exercising free will. This is a fact because couples decide when to have sex; they don't get into a trance and then suddenly find themselves copulating.

It is simply unwise for a couple to have a number of children which is too large to sustain; apart from insufficient financial capacity, it may not be possible to give individualised attention in mentoring each of the children. In this modern busy world, it is obvious that when a person has a large family, he will not effectively keep guard of each child's behaviour and his or her physical, mental, and social needs. Clearly, it is this inability that makes many fathers of large families to be out of touch with the lives of their children; out of a family will be different characters for which a father has no idea of how each one lives his or her life.

Now, how true is it that family planning is wrong because it prevents children who are *"gifts from God"* from getting born? And, is it true that family planning by use of condoms is sinful because it wastes (kills) children in the sheath? Well, consider the following facts:

- When a male ejaculates into a woman's vagina, semen is released. That semen contains millions and millions of sperms. However, only one is able to meet and fertilise the egg. The rest of the sperms are unsuccessful, will pour out of the vagina and die off. It is interesting to note here that the vagina's environment is acidic and this kills the sperm. So, if you don't practise family planning for fear of killing sperm in a condom, be informed that the vagina's acidic environment also kills the sperm. So, whether in the condom or in the vagina, sperm will still die. Furthermore, even when a woman conceives there is still the death of sperm which could not meet the egg.

- A sperm is not a child. A child is a human being whose formation only begins when two entities, the sperm and egg, combine. To say a sperm is a child is as wrong as regarding the element hydrogen to be water simply because it is part of the atoms which make up water – hydrogen and oxygen (H_2O). Water is only water when the two elements are present and combined. In their separate states – hydrogen or oxygen – are not water: they each are completely different in their properties.

- In light of the above facts, to answer the question of whether the use of condoms is right or wrong, ask yourself this: is the death of unsuccessful sperm in the vagina different from the death of sperm trapped in the condom? Is it not clear that the sperm which gets trapped in a condom ends up dying just like the one which failed to fertilise the egg despite having entered the vagina without the barrier of a condom?

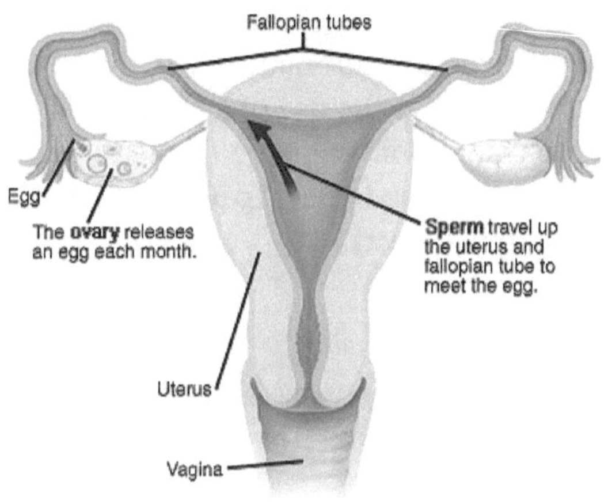

Female sexual organ

Now, why do some Christians have a negative perception of condoms? On two occasions I have heard men say, *"Why use condoms when you are married?"* This question expresses a common misunderstanding about condoms: a condom is commonly perceived as a tool for committing fornication because many people use it for promiscuity. However, it is also important to consider the fact that there are married couples who use condoms for their family planning. It should be simple to understand that if two persons are married there is no sin in them having sex. Sin has nothing to do with the plastic worn on the penis but everything to do with the state of the relationship between a man and a woman engaged in the act of sexual intercourse. When a married couple engage in sex it is not sinful because they are practising it in the state of being married. However, the same act of sex would be sinful if it involved individuals who are not married. It therefore goes without saying that the use of a condom is right or wrong depending on the state of the sexual act in which it is being used. (See **Appendix III** for other details on this subject).

Genesis 38:9

Now, what about this verse and what has it got to do with family planning? The verse reads:

> *And Judah said unto Onan, Go in unto thy brother's wife, and marry her, and raise up seed to thy brother. And Onan knew that the seed should not be his; and it came to pass, when he went in unto his brother's wife, that he spilled it on the ground, lest that he should give seed to his brother.*

Is it correct to suggest that God killed the man in this verse because of his sole act of spilling the sperm on the ground? Not so. A simple reading of the verse should let us know that the act of spilling the sperm should not be looked at in isolation; the whole context of the story should be considered. The man was given to marry the woman for the purpose of giving her children in the place of his brother. If he never wanted this arrangement he should have refused from taking her as wife. But his thoughts were mischievous; he had already determined in his heart not to give the woman children (contrary to the agreement) but he still went ahead to have sex with her and spilled his seed to the ground *"lest that he should give seed to his brother."* It is this wickedness of heart that displeased God.

3. **"My husband and I are both in employment but yet are always broke. This situation many times makes us to argue and quarrel. His uncles, nephews, grandparents, and siblings are always asking for money and he doesn't seem to know the words, 'Sorry, I am not able to help this time'. He will give them money even when we are in need of it at home. I know we ought to help our families but should it be done at the expense of our family's joy?"**

This is a legitimate concern that affects many couples. May I first point out the various factors that can cause financial problems in a family:

- *Spending money without having a carefully worked out budget.*

Many times couples who do this become victims of the modern day deceivableness of business advertisements which can excite a person into spending money on things which may not even be necessary to buy. If most such couples would stop and give even a little thought about what they want to impulsively buy, they would reconsider and instead opt to save their hard earned money.

- *Getting into debts.*

A person who gets into a habit of borrowing money will soon or later become a victim of stress. This stress will later *spread* to the wife and children as they will slowly get affected by the lack of resources in the house.

There was a time when Norah and I would always find our money depleting even before we used it on important needs. The strain was so much that we could not even remain with spare cash for buying clothes, or enjoying a good time with the family. I began to realise that the absence of money in the home invited stress and tension. This was not good. I told Norah:

You know what, we work a whole month to earn this money and we can't just be giving it away; Lets clear off all debts in the next two to three months, and then restart on a note of spending according to budget. Secondly, let's open a bank account where a fixed amount will be getting deposited for our monthly savings. Thirdly, let's also agree on an amount to put aside every month which will be used for responding to financial requests from relatives. We will strictly be helping them from this allotment and not money meant for our family's savings.

We were happy at the plan and started disciplining ourselves to adhere to it. In about eight months' time there was quite a change. I realised that we had even gained some little body weight as the stress subsided. We became happier and there was almost a continuous sense of peace and joy between us. This let me know that many problems of tension, anger and frustrations can be avoided by having a sound financial policy in the house.

- *Helping relatives and other people at the expense of your family.*

This is not right. A husband's wife and children should take first priority in the manner he spends money. We have two hands and not four hands, and two legs and not four legs, for a purpose; much as we would love to help and should help people, let us also be aware that we cannot help the whole world. As a couple do what you can to help people but not at the expense of the joy of your family.

Now, please take note that as a wife you may not be in a good position to address these sensitive concerns to your husband; doing that may only provoke an agitated negative reaction. More prudent to do will be the two of you to start investing time in attending good couples' meetings where such things are taught; an example is the bi-monthly *Believers Couples Fellowship* held at Believers' Assembly.[17] Alternatively, invest time in jointly reading books like this one with your husband. Above all, commit the matter in prayer.

4. ***"My wife seems to be never interested in sex. We only have it a few times and she doesn't seem to fully participate in those moments. I feel starved. What can I do for her to be in love with me?"***

Several things could lead to this problem. Which of the following do you think may apply to your situation:

- *You don't show affection to your wife by way of making her feel loved and appreciated.*

A husband can show affection towards his wife in different ways: speaking to her about how you appreciate her and how she is special to you, taking her out for lunch; spending time with her as your love, etc. This is what wins a woman's heart to her man, not sex. If you are not closely bonded in fellowship and you only smile to her when you want sex in bed, she will feel that you don't love her but are only interested in her body. Of great importance to know here is that whilst males get attracted to women by sight, females are

---

[17] For more information about these meetings contact: *voiceoftheword@live.com.*

different; a woman's love and attachment to a man develops through his show of affection towards her.

- *Having a wife who is very busy and stressed with work.*

There are now many marriages in which both the husband and wife are engaged in employment. This is mainly due to the ever rising cost of living. There are now many financial challenges involved in managing a family. Now, much as having a wife who is work-engaged can help reduce the couple's financial burden, it is wise for a man to realise that there is an extra-workload on the woman who still has to continue with house chores after knocking off from work. Is it not strange that immediately after reaching home the woman may start cooking, doing laundry, or bath the kids? Take note that in many homes (at least in Zambia) as the "*weaker vessel*" will be performing all these tasks the stronger one will be relaxing in the sofa, reading a newspaper or changing channels on TV. When it is time to go to bed, the man would have refreshed whilst his lady is all tired.

It is wise for a man to realise that the day's job at his wife's company could have been enough to tire her, and the extra workload at home only makes it worse. I often advise couples in such situations to employ one or two maids to assist with work around the house. Remember that Sarah, Abraham's wife, also had a maid to perform work on her behalf (Genesis 16:1). This is the Sarah who called her husband "*Lord*", not because he treated her as a slave, but because he regarded her as his queen. Abraham could not abuse his beloved queen with stressful work; he let her have a maid. I trust it would be a noble thing for men to emulate Abraham, the great patriarch of our faith.

With a maid to help your wife, she will have time to relax and recuperate before going to bed. The woman will also be healthier and happier. In this way she may also not feel too tired for sex.

- *Having a wife who is moody and simply neglecting her conjugal duties.*

There are some women who don't know one thing about giving respect to their husbands and who would take it for granted to starve a man of the love he needs from his wife.

I once had an unpleasant counselling session where a couple sat before me and the woman would intermittently and rudely interrupt her husband as he complained about her lack of respect and starving him of sex. Looking at the woman, as she did her best to defend herself, a verse came to my mind: "*Every wise woman buildeth her house: but the foolish plucketh it down with her hands*" (Proverbs 14:1). Any wise woman should know that sex plays an important role in marriage. However, it is not something that should be merely taken as a role; it should proceed from love. Apostle Paul admonished: "*Let the husband render unto the wife due benevolence: and likewise also the wife unto the husband. The wife hath not power of her own body, but the husband: and likewise also the husband hath not power of his own body, but the wife. Defraud ye not one the other, except it be with consent for a time, that ye may give yourselves to fasting and prayer; and come together again, that Satan tempt you not for your incontinency"* (1 Corinthians 7:3-5).

- *Sexual dysfunction*

The term *sexual dysfunction* is used to describe sets of conditions that can affect a person's sexual life. Sexual Dysfunction can reduce one's desire to have sex or failing to get aroused during sex; it can lead to failure to reach orgasm or having premature ejaculations. There are some known conditions or diseases (e.g. diabetes) that can cause this condition (see **Appendix I** - *Diseases that can affect a couple's sexual life*). I advise that you seek medical advice on how such conditions can be rectified.

THE ABOVE LIST IS not exhaustive; it merely serves to illustrate the different things that can cause the problem of a wife being not interested in sex. I should stress that marital problems can never be solved with an arithmetical approach of "do *this* for *that* to happen". Marriage is a relationship that is not mainly based on logic but love and emotions. One needs to be wise, patient and above all, prayerful. God's Word admonishes us that *"in everything by prayer and supplication with thanksgiving let your requests be made known unto God"* (Philippians 4:6).

5. ***"My husband always chats with a female friend on the phone. He is ever on WhatsApp talking to her. When I confront him about it, he always explains that it is a business partner he is talking to. My worry is that he is ever so protective of his phone. He cannot leave it behind or allow me to touch or make a call using his phone. When I request for his phone to make a call, he would rather give me money to buy airtime and use my phone. My worries once heightened, when I once overhead him say (in a low-tone voice), 'I miss you' to someone I suspected to be the lady he is flirting with. How do I handle this situation seeing that I can't approach him over a matter I don't have concrete evidence?"***

When you see a man behaving in the following ways, with regards his phone, then chances are that he is in an inappropriate relationship with another woman:[18]

• Always keeping guard of the phone and feeling insecure when it is in the hands of the spouse.

---

[18] Men are the ones often in this kind of behaviour although some women are also capable of such behaviour.

The person just can't leave the phone behind; he carries it even to the toilet - while the wife thinks the husband is doing what normally happens in the water closet, the idiot could be busy texting love messages.

• Ever chatting on social media with someone but for whom the inbox is always empty. Chances are that the *cheater* keeps deleting chat messages. Shrewder *cheaters* would even save the number of a secret lover with a male name to give an impression that they are not chatting with a female. Oh, what wickedness and deceptiveness!

• Keeping the phone in silence-mode but which keeps receiving text messages. The person is probably receiving continuous chat messages but for which he wants to prevent his wife from suspecting what is going on.

Many times the above suspicions turn out to be true. May I say this: a man or woman, who cheats on his wife or husband, by having an extra-marital affair, is a wicked hypocrite whose reasoning has stopped functioning and is now being led by the filth of lust. Lust blinds such a person so much that he won't see the impending terrible loss of joy and peace that will plague both himself and his own children. The hurt done to his spouse will be so devastating, and the resulting damage and mistrust can be irreparable. Much as there have been cases of such unfortunate situations being caused by a woman who is not fulfilling her duties to the man, there are simply no logical grounds for promiscuity. Promiscuity is a dirty thing which must never be tolerated or entertained. The trouble is, once a person indulges in the first act of promiscuity it later becomes a habit which is very hard to get away from.

Now, to answer the question of what you can do about such a situation given that there is no "concrete" evidence, first, please know that in marriage there should be no room for 'political correctness' like one often displayed in court-rooms where even when a judge can see the guilt in the person's eyes he has to rely on the so-called evidence-based facts. Second, there is a gradual solution which has proved to work for some couples I have counselled.

- *No room for political correctness in marriage.*

A marriage should be governed by sincerity and trust founded on the standard of God's Word. The problem is that many marriages did not start in Christ. In a Christian marriage, when you begin to experience symptoms of infidelity from your husband or wife, understand that Satan is attempting to invade your home and a hurricane of problems are on their way. You first have to approach the matter with earnest prayer and fasting, seeking the intervention of God. Ask God to give you wisdom, then approach your husband with respect, sincerity, and calmness. Let him know your concerns. Don not ask with confrontation. Confrontation has never solved a problem; it only awakes a person's ego to become defensive. If your husband is a believer, I trust that if you handle the matter with God on your side and with respect, victory will come your way. However, if he is a hypocrite who only shows up at church once in a while and is in a habit of promiscuity, the solution may not be easy. However, there is a gradual solution that has worked for some couples:

- *With your husband, invest time in regularly attending couples meetings like the Believers Couples Fellowship meetings.*

A person who spends three years of time at a good School of Engineering ultimately becomes a good engineer; another who learns engineering on the streets may try to fix a few things *here* and *there* but will only have mediocre skills of trying out things by trial and error. This applies to all other forms of profession; a person who gets trained is more likely to do good quality work. Some training take as long as three to four years. Now, is it not interesting to note that many human beings spend countless years in a classroom to get equipped to join institutions of employment where their skills will be applied, but yet do not invest any little time whatsoever in knowledge that will guide them in the institution of marriage where they will spend their entire life? It is little wonder the 'profession' of marriage has the highest number of failures.

At Believers' Assembly we have a bi-monthly couples' fellowship where various important topics about marriage are taught. The meetings are spruced with assignments and interesting practical activities to help couples experience the joy of marriage. We believe that what a mind continuously hears and associates with, it gradually becomes. Thus, a man who is ever found in a wrong company of friends who are not spiritual and have ill-advice on matters of marriage, will eventually adopt wrong attitudes which will negatively impact his marriage. Likewise a marriage that constantly feeds itself with sound advice will gradually be transformed into a sound union. I believe it is because of this process that some couples at BFC have experienced reconciliation, healing and the restoration of joy in their marriages. Such meetings produce tremendous results as they work to routinely subject couple's minds to knowledge about a successful marriage. A typical BFC meeting starts with a teaching to be followed by a sharing of a testimony by an invited elderly couple. At the end of the testimony, couples in the audience can ask questions (synonymously). Later, group discussions on given topics are held. A meeting concludes with praying for various marital prayer requests. Make efforts to encourage your spouse to attend such meetings together. The results may not be instant but will certainly gradually manifest.

6. *"My relatives do not get along with my wife. They say that since she came into*

my life I have stopped being supportive of the family. And I have noticed that whenever my mother and siblings visit our home, my wife always gets moody because of mom who always wants to advise her on various things - how to manage a home, how to cook, etc. I feel my wife gets intimidated at this but she has a problem of not opening up to me. What can I do?"

There are some cases of mean wives who are so egocentric and create home environments which are so unwelcoming to relatives. Men who are married to such women are in deep trouble. However, in reading between the lines of what you have written, your wife doesn't seem to fit this category of wild cats. There seems to be nothing wrong with your wife but much wrong with the attitude of your family towards your wife. Even so, much of the problem is with you. You are a king who lets his queen get desecrated in her own castle! I am afraid you are destroying your marriage with the support of your family but without knowing what you are doing.

Kindly understand this: A marriage ceremony is not the uniting of two families to become one big entity. This is a misconception, especially in Africa where when two people get married, some relatives and siblings see it as a new avenue for requesting financial assistance. Let us understand that when two people get married, it is them – the bride and groom – who have become one and have formed a new entity in society whose independence should be respected. Their new home will have expenses and commitments which either individual had not experienced before getting into the marriage. The new couple will be faced with new expenses: rent, food budget, school fees for their children, and miscellaneous other burdens. This is the simple reason why you can no longer help your family in the same way you use to when you were single! "*But they don't understand that!*", some in similar situations have exclaimed to me: Well, who said that one is under obligation to make them understand that? Should a person ruin his marriage on the expense of his relatives' ignorance or their lack of empathy?

My bigger worry and concern about your situation is that as a husband you are not in control and haven't put protection on your wife. Surely, how can your mother begin to counsel your wife about how to manage a home, and how to cook?[19] Where did she get the courage? Relatives will behave in a home according to the level of tolerance which has been given to them. If they disrespect and demean your wife, it is you who is responsible

---

[19] Some elderly and friendly mothers-in-law get sweetly along with their daughters-in-law and would enjoy each other's company. In such a set-up, there would be nothing offensive if a mother-in-law were to exclaim, "*Hey dear, let me show you a way of cooking this, you will love the yummy taste!*" A wise elderly woman knows how to teach a lesson to a younger woman with *tact* and *diplomacy*!

for their freedom to do such. And think about this: if your relatives have the audacity to treat your wife the way they are doing now, how would they treat her if you were to die and leave her behind? Certainly, she will be at their disposal for all manner of exploitation and abuse. Such are families which cannot wait to claim properties of the deceased. Listen: a man who doesn't put the protection of respect upon his wife and does not present her as a queen to his family, is leaving his wife in a lot of problems if he happens to die.

It is a man's duty to ensure that their marriage union is allocated first priority in terms of financial, moral, and spiritual support. Let us look at each of these crucial issues in a little more detail:

- *Financial* support

It should never be mandatory for a husband or wife to give financial support to their relatives. The couple should give financial assistance to relatives out of their own free will and within their capacity. I am aware that this may be a strange concept for an African society where the words "family" or "brotherhood" are grossly abused to mean free unconditional support for relatives. Unless this mind-set changes, Africa will continue to nurture societies of people who live below their potential because of the 'dependence' syndrome. I know of a friend who always wants to respond to financial requests from his family even when his own wife and children do not have enough money for clothing, food, and other needs. That is simply not a wise thing to do.

I know of a man who lives abroad in a prosperous country. Some years back, when I was young, one would think people were writing letters to God when they would write one letter after the other, asking for various forms of assistance from him: from requests for school fees for one's own children to any clothes the man was no longer using! I have to admit that I admire the big heart of the man; he never gets tired to help family members. However, there are many times I felt his help was bread thrown to waste. Well, with time he has changed his style: he now gives interest-free loans instead of free cash. This change has obviously angered some people. But, I would say that he is now doing the right thing as that will make people be aware that regardless of where one is, whether in London or Lusaka, money doesn't drop from heaven. People ought to realise that the world owes them nothing; everyone has to work hard in order to survive.

- *Moral support*

As a husband you ought to provide moral support to your wife. Let her feel your confidence in her. Show her that you respect and adore her.

On 29th August, 2015, I pulled a surprise event called *Matebeto*. This is a traditional ceremony in my country which is performed by the wife's relatives for her husband to show appreciation for the latter. However, on that date I broke tradition and instead did it for my wife. As I began inviting relatives to the event, many exclaimed with surprise as others dismissed it as being "Odd". Well, on that day, as anxiety turned into anticipation and anticipation into an exuberant celebration, the main activity of the even took place: a speech in which I demonstrated that a man's headship over a woman doesn't mean she should to be treated like a doormat. Here tradition was broken on purpose to let couples in my family and also at church know that Norah occupies first place in my life before anyone else, and I hoped that this would inspire husbands to take care of their wives.

As a husband let your wife know that she is your first priority in terms of love or financial support. When she is speaking to you, learn to quietly listen and show that you value her words. Doing this will not reduce your status of being head of the family in any way. Actually, it will make your wife respect you more. Again, this does not mean that you won't have misunderstandings with your wife. As long as you are creatures of brains with red blood cells running through your veins, disagreements and misunderstandings will be there. However, what distinguishes mature couples from childish ones is the manner in which misunderstandings are handled.

Maturity in marriage has nothing to do with how huge and big a person's body looks. There are many big-looking married folk but who have little or no sense of wisdom in the way they handle their marital problems. A wise and mature couple will never express their anger at each other in public, not even in the presence of their children; whatever misunderstanding or disagreement they may have will be sorted out privately. In public (and by this I don't mean in a stadium or auditorium but in the presence of any third-part entity including siblings or parents) a couple should show one face and people ought to give due respect to that *face*!

• *Spiritual support*

As a husband, apart from seeing the woman you married as your wife, be aware that she is also a daughter of God. She is not some piece of property that you bought from her relatives! She is an entity made in the image and likeness of God, valued not in terms of the bride price you paid but by the token of the Blood of the Lord Jesus Christ which was shed for her salvation. So, much as the husband is the head over a wife, he ought to treat her with love, adoration and spiritual care, as a precious gift from God. *"A prudent wife is from the LORD"*, says the Scripture (Proverbs 19:14). A sober woman will not take the husband's respectful treatment of her for granted by becoming unsubmissive; that will be quite illogical! Her husband's good attitude towards her will actually inspire and enthuse her to respect him more. The saying is true that when you treat your wife like a queen she will treat you like a king.

So, in conclusion, to answer the question *"What can I do?"* I would say: Create an environment in your home where people will begin to give respect to your *queen*. If your relatives do not like how she cooks certain food, let them eat elsewhere; they should never use shortcomings of your wife as their gateway to scorn or scold her. That is just plain wrong. Let them know that what angers her will anger you. They ought to see you as one, and not a favourable piece that belongs to them but which was mended to a stranger.

Appendices

I.　Diseases that can affect a couple's sexual life.

There are different health challenges, conditions, or diseases that can appear in marriage which can negatively affect the general welfare and sexual life of a couple. The term *sexual dysfunction* is used to describe sets of conditions that can affect a person's sexual life. Sexual Dysfunction can reduce one's desire to have sex or failing to get aroused during sex; it can lead to failure to reach orgasm or having premature ejaculations.

This article is very brief as it only aims to awaken you to the need to be health-conscious. Let me put the health problems in two categories – those often caused by circumstances beyond one's control and those which can arise out of a careless lifestyle. This is not a formal or technical distinction; I use it here just for purposes of structuring this discussion.

- *Health problems most likely caused by circumstances beyond one's control.*

Sex plays an important role in marriage. However, misfortune can occur which incapacitates one spouse from being sexually active. Such an unfortunate situation can be caused by different eventualities such as the development of a disease caused by a genetic disorder (e.g. hereditary prostate cancer[20]) or incapacitation caused by an accident. If a couple happens to find themselves in such a painful situation, their love, care and empathy should manifest to the maximum. The spouse who is fine should accept the situation and willingly help the affected one in carrying the burden. Instead of entertaining depression (which often leads to more other problems), the healthy spouse should strengthen himself or herself and use the situation as an opportunity to triumph in the trial of their faith. The spouse who is fine should express deep love for the sick one, letting him or her know that regardless of what has happened to their body, it is the person inside the body that they are in love with and got married to. It is here that true love between spouses can be tested.

It is amazing how some couples have overcome some eventualities, especially of cancer, which has become a prevalent problem. If you are in a marriage which is suffering from the challenge of cancer please take time to read these insightful testimonies and articles about how you can manage your situation: *FACING CANCER AS A COUPLE* by Nancie Christie (Christie, 2015) and *HOW CANCER CAN AFFECT YOUR SEXUALITY AND SEX LIFE* by the Cancer Research UK (2015). These

---

[20] Please note that like all other cancers it is not easy to pin point the cause of prostate cancer. However, what leads to the growth of the cancerous cells is a mutation that occurs in a person's DNA. It has been noted that some prostate cancer patients inherited the genetic disorder that causes the disease(Ellis, 2014).

articles are available online and should be found with a simple Google search.

* *Diseases caused by careless lifestyles*

Much as there are unfortunate health conditions caused by genetic disorders or other circumstances beyond one's control, we should also be aware that there are equally many health problems which are a result of careless lifestyles, such as the eating of wrong foods or the lack of doing exercises. Some of these diseases can badly impair a couple's sexual life. One common example of such a disease is diabetes, an illness that today affects a lot of people in Zambia and many other countries around the world.

Diabetes is a harmful condition which can damage blood vessels and nerves that control the erection of a penis. Studies have shown that a lot of men with diabetes risk developing *erectile dysfunction* (impotence), a condition in which a man fails to maintain an erection long enough during sexual intercourse. Diabetes arises as a result of a disorder in the way a body uses the food which has been digested for energy. When we eat foods which are rich in carbohydrates, the digestion process in our body breaks it down to *glucose*. Glucose is the form in which sugar exists in our blood stream. Cells in the body use this glucose for their energy. A substance known as *insulin* is what causes the cells to be able to absorb the glucose. Diabetes develops when a body has little insulin to perform this task, or when the insulin is present but is interfered from working properly. Note that there are different kinds of diabetes just as there are different causes of it. However, here we are interested in the type that is most common. It is called *Type 2 Diabetes*.

Type 2 Diabetes *"develops most often in middle-aged and older people who are also overweight or obese"* notes the National Institute of Diabetes and Digestive and Kidney Diseases (NIDDK, 2016). This disease occurs when there is no balance between the intake of calories and bodily exercise which should lead to the consumption of the glucose that result from the calories:

> *An imbalance between caloric intake and physical activity can lead to obesity, which causes insulin resistance and is common in people with Type 2 Diabetes. Central obesity, in which a person has excess abdominal fat, is a major risk factor not only for insulin resistance and Type 2 Diabetes but also for heart and blood vessel disease, also called cardiovascular disease (CVD). This excess 'belly fat' produces hormones and other substances that can cause harmful, chronic effects in the body such as damage to blood vessels* (NIDDK, 2016).

The good news is that this disease can be prevented: *"studies show that millions of people can lower their risk for Type 2 Diabetes by making lifestyle changes and losing weight."*

It's a relief to know that some of these terrible diseases which can rob a couple of the joy of marriage can actually be controlled by adopting a lifestyle of discipline. Cleveland Clinic (2016) has published an easy to read and understand article on other diseases that can lead to Sexual Dysfunction, and some ways of preventing them. One condition the article discusses is cardiovascular disease, including high blood pressure, hypertension and peripheral vascular diseases. These conditions damage blood vessels which supply blood to organs of the body. One such organs are genitals – the penis in males and vagina in females. The damage to the blood vessels results into less blood flowing to the genitals. This condition in turn makes a person fail to get sexually aroused during intercourse.

For treatment of cardiovascular diseases seek medical advice. However, experts have frequently advised adopting healthy lifestyles including eating a healthy diet, getting regular exercises, and being physically active. Besides this, it is important to take interest to research on health matters. Many people take matters of health with an indifferent attitude but not until they get affected. But be wise, prevention is always better than cure. The Scripture admonishes us that our bodies are temples of the Holy Spirit and so we ought to take care of them. (1 Corinthians 6:19). Some websites that can help you on matters of health include: *my.clevelandclinic.org,* *www.webmd.com,* *www.heart.org,* and *www.niddk.nih.gov.*

II. Benefits of planning

Three important benefits of planning include the following:

It:

- *Enables you to focus and avoid time-wasting activities.*

A person without a plan is like a stray dog which embarks on a journey to go to a place but no sooner does it smell an appetising smell than it changes direction to follow the smell. In reality there are some people like that. You can actually detect such a lifestyle in a person by observing the way they live their daily life: they cannot concentrate on an activity; they easily get tossed to and fro by distractions that come their way. A friend can show up and ask them, *"Would you escort me to such and such a place"*, and they will gladly offer the escort. Another one can later find them free again and ask them to give an escort and they will gladly offer company. This is not the way of a focussed person. A focussed person plans his or her day ahead and hence keeps away from activities that don't add value to the objectives set for the day.

- *Enables you to allocate your resources where they are needed most.*

Without a plan resources can be allocated towards activities that do not yield meaningful benefit. But when you invest time in planning, you would have thoroughly thought through projects or activities that really need attention.

* *Prepares you to meet and contain problems you had anticipated but for which you already set contingent plans.*

One important step in planning is to try to think about the different problems that can happen in a given situation and what would be the possible solution for each problem. This is very important. A person who does not take time to ponder about possible problems that can occur, will often be in a state of helplessness when an unexpected event occurs. On the other hand, a person who thought through what could possibly happen would have prepared contingency plans of what to do in case of an eventuality. Many people are familiar with this concept when it comes to compulsory things such as motor vehicle insurance but yet they make no effort to plan ahead for the safety of their family. However, there are some who do. For example, a responsible husband will take time to think about what would happen if his employment contract got terminated unexpectedly. He will think about investments to make *now* that can sustain his family if his job were to end or if he were to unexpectedly die. These are not nice things to think or talk about but they nevertheless happen to every human being and so common sense demands that a person should prepare for them.

- *Motivates you to keep pursuing set goals and objectives.*

Time can be full of discouragements and distractions. However, a person who wakes up each day knowing that he only has a little time to be alive on earth soon finds himself compelled to put himself together to continue pursuing the tasks he needs to accomplish. This is similar to what keeps people running in a race. What keeps them running is not the enjoyment of running itself but the goal or reward of the race. It is for this reason that one can fall down but still get up and continue running. One needs to get up and keep focussing on the goal of the race. In likening our spiritual lives to a race the writer of the epistle to the Hebrews in the Bible encouraged them to *"run with patience the race that is set before us"* (Hebrews 12:1).

- *Enables you to measure, monitor, evaluate, and control your progress.*

Without set goals or targets, a person has nothing by which to measure progress. A written list of items which ought to be accomplished within a specified time-frame can work as a checklist for monitoring progress. If progress is not occurring according to plan a person can try to evaluate where resources have been wrongly spent. The information gathered can be used to implement controls that will align activities according to what was planned.

III. *"I will multiply thy conception"*

Human beings are the only creatures experiencing great difficult in determining when they intend to have children. This is because the female has an *increased* possibility of conceiving, about once every 28 days. We are informed in the Bible that this came as a result of the Original Sin when the woman (Eve) succumbed to the serpent's deception:[21]

> *Unto the woman He said, I will greatly multiply thy sorrow and thy conception; in sorrow thou shalt bring forth children; and thy desire shall be to thy husband, and he shall rule over thee* (Genesis 3:16).

Two things were multiplied: first, the sorrow (pain) of conception, and second, the number of times that a woman can conceive. The number of times is a cycle of about 28 days once every month. It is known as *menstruation*. During this period a woman indeed happens to go through the sorrow of distress. Now, it should be pointed out here that it is this curse which brought about the difficulty of trying to balance between having sex for pleasure and for conceiving a child. So, for those who oppose family planning as being ungodly, does it mean that because the "increase of conception" came as a

---

[21] For a detailed discourse on this subject read this author's book titled *FORBIDDEN THEOLOGY: Making sense of the Genesis story* (available on www.amazon.com).

result of God's punishment then couples should be letting their every sexual act to lead to conception? That would surely lead to abnormally large families, and that will be actually adding more pain to the punishment. Consider this: At the same time the judgement of conception was pronounced on the woman, the following was also said to her husband:

> *And unto Adam he said, Because thou hast hearkened unto the voice of thy wife, and hast eaten of the tree, of which I commanded thee, saying, Thou shalt not eat of it: cursed is the ground for thy sake; in sorrow shalt thou eat of it all the days of thy life* (Genesis 3:17).

Now, does this cursing of the ground by God mean that it is a sin for a farmer to apply fertiliser to the soil to enable it to produce a better yield? Surely, not so. The very problem of now having to add fertiliser is part of the cost we are bearing as a consequence of the sin. Likewise, although sicknesses came as a result of the Fall in the beginning, we (just like some Biblical saints did) still use medicine to help us survive the consequences of the Original Sin. It would be ridiculous for a believer to explain that because sickness came as a result of God's judgement in the beginning it therefore would be wrong to use medicine to counter diseases. It goes without saying that it is equally unwise for a couple to avoid family planning on the premise that the increased conception in women came as a result of God's judgement. A husband and wife who would follow such a belief to the letter would certainly create a bizarre family:[22] as afore-stated it would mean letting each act of sex lead to a pregnancy.

IV.   Inspired by the Singapore story

In December 2014 through January 2015, I had a busy missionary itinerary which stretched from the Philippines through Singapore to Cambodia. Philippines and Cambodia seemed to me (in some ways) to be another version of Africa – noisy cities and bus-stops, street vending and unkempt buildings and surroundings. But Singapore, the little tiny country, yet a formidable economic giant which is among the most prosperous countries in the world, gave me quite a different experience altogether.

As I went around the different places of the city-state, riding from one electric train to another, and visiting some eating places and shops, I wondered how a country could be this orderly. For a moment, I remembered words of an economist whom I once heard explaining that it is a mistake to compare a poor African country to a developed one of the West because the poor country may have a very young history compared to that of the developed one which may have taken years to reach where it is. *"50 year old Zambia can't be compared to USA which is over 200 years old"*, the man

------

[22] A couple following such a flawed belief should not even use the natural method of family planning as that would amount to the sin of preventing the conception of children.

explained. The explanation was convincing and I believed it, but not until this moment when I was in a country which not only got independent at the same time like Zambia but was once a decrepit economy whose future rested on a razor-edge of uncertainty but yet is today a First World nation.

Singapore's independence was not one which had been fought for; the country was asked to leave the Federation of Malaysia because of its disagreements and antagonism over the policies of the federal government. By being alienated Singapore was now to stay on its own. This was a 'death sentence' imposed on Singapore; a total disaster which was too heavy to announce to the country; the Prime Minister sobbed in public as he struggled to break the news to the citizens of the new country. This little nation, unlike Zambia, had no natural resources to survive on. News media predicted its soon collapse. There were tremendous odds to be overcome. Reading the story of how the country rose from being a swampy island to a metropolis of skyscrapers almost sounds like fiction, but it happened.

The question is: how could a country the same age as Zambia be way ahead in everything. The answer lies in one man whose impeccable leadership wit, integrity, and charisma transformed the city-state, not by first constructing roads and buildings but by changing the mind-set of Singaporeans; he did not accomplish this by making formal cold and indifferent speeches but by heartily communicating to the citizens the need to change behaviour at personal and family levels. He was determined to make a First World country in a Third World region. He believed that the lack of resources would not determine the fate of Singapore. As Henry Kissinger once commented about the economic challenges during the early post-independence years of Singapore, *"Superior intelligence, discipline and ingenuity would substitute for resources."*[23]

Despite his country being in a hopeless state, it is interesting to note how Mr Lee didn't go to seek for aid from wealthy nations; in his memoirs he recounted:

> *I was convinced our people must never have an aid-dependent mentality. If we had to succeed we had to depend on ourselves...Next, assistance should provide Singapore with jobs through industries and not make us dependent on perpetual injections of aid. I warned our workers, 'The world does not owe us a living. We cannot live by the begging bowl'*
> (Lee, 2000).

One important strategy that Mr Lee embarked on, which I believe contributed immensely to the success story of Singapore, was the control he put on population growth. People were encouraged to only have up to two children. The simple logic is that the world has limited resources but which are

---

[23] Stated in his foreword in Lee Kuan Yew's *FROM THIRD WORLD TO FIRST* (Lee,2000).

required to satisfy potentially unlimited wants. *"Wants"* are contained in human beings. These human beings do not just pop into existence; they come from a wilful desire by a couple to produce children. Thus, excessive consumption of resources which can naturally be caused by having an excessive number of people can be controlled by having a population which is in reasonable proportion to its limited resources. This is a basic principle of economics which most leaders in poor countries don't seem to grasp. Just compare the population-growths of Zambia and Singapore in the past 50 years:

Country	*Year:* **1965**	*Year:* **2015**
Singapore	2 million	5 million
Zambia	4 million	15 million

These are approximations of population data. See actual figures in the World Bank's Population Data (World Bank, 2016).

Notice how in fifty years' time Singapore's population has only grown about one place upwards and that of poor Zambia has swelled about three times more than its original size! However, the important difference between the two countries lies not in the population numbers *per se* but in the kinds of leadership at the helm of political power. Let us understand that no matter how a country can be populated with intelligent people if the instruments of power are in the hands of nincompoops, mediocrity reigns. And, it is said that an army of lions which is led by a sheep will be defeated by an army of sheep led by a lion. So, contrary to popular opinion, development does not begin with resources; it begins with **wisdom** in a leader who is able to interpret the environment of his people and then provide a **strategic plan** which will set the **direction** of what people should aspire for. In a family unit the leader is the father of the house. A wise father should be determined never to live a life of excuses. He is ultimately responsible for the challenges of his family and he should work to provide inspiring leadership that should secure a sound future for his family.

A.C. Phiri is pastor of ***Believers' Assembly***, a non-denominational church in Zambia, where Christians seeking in-depth Bible study, prayer and fellowship gather to worship. Andrew has spoken and taught in various meetings and conferences in Africa and overseas including Singapore, the Philippines, India, Cambodia, Namibia, Uganda, Zimbabwe, Malawi and Mozambique. He takes keen interest in missionary work and helping the poor in rural villages of Africa.

Other books by the same author

WHY I BELIEVE GOD EXISTS
Discourse on the scientific evidence

FORBIDDEN THEOLOGY
Making sense of the Genesis story

Available on www.amazon.com

References

Alleyne, R. (2011). Food for thought: Diet does boost your intelligence. *The Telegraph*.[Online] Available from: http://www.telegraph.co.uk/news/health/news/8308726/Food-for-thought-diet-does-boost-your-intelligence.html. [Accessed 10th February, 2016].

Branham, W. M. (1957). *Time Tested Memorials of God*. Indiana, USA: Voice of God Recordings.

Branham, W.M. (1957). *Hebrews Part III. Indiana, USA:* Voice of God Recordings.

Branham, W.M. (1965). *The Choosing of a Bride*. Indiana, USA: Voice of God Recordings.

Britten, B. and Britten, C. (2003). *Answers for your Marriage*. Florida: Worldwide Books.

Britten, B. and Britten, C. (2003). *Answers for your Marriage*. Gweru, Zimbabwe: Mambo Press.

Cancer Research UK (2015). *How cancer can affect your sexuality and sex life* .[Online] Available from: http://www.cancerresearchuk.org/about-cancer/coping-with-cancer/coping-physically/sex-sexuality-and-cancer/how-cancer-can-affect-your-sexuality-and-sex-life. [Accessed 18th February, 2016].

Cleveland Clinic (2016). *Sexual Dysfunction and Disease*. [Online] Available from: https://my.clevelandclinic.org/health/disease

s_conditions/hic_An_Overview_of_Sexual_D ysfunction/hic_Sexual_Dysfunction_and_Dis ease. [Accessed: 19th February, 2016].

Coory, D.(2009). *Secrets of Fascinating Womanhood*. New Zealand: Zealand Publishing House.

Cox, F.D. (2002). *Human Intimacy: Marriage, the Family, and Its Meaning (9the Ed)*. Australia: Wadsworth.

Ellis, M.E. (2014). *Causes and risks of Prostate Cancer*. [Online] Available from: http://www.healthline.com/health/prostate-cancer-risk-factors#Overview1. [Accessed 18th February, 2016].

Lee, K. Y. (2000). *From Third World To First: The Singapore Story: 1965-2000*. Singapore: Marshal Cavendish Editions.

Lewis, C.S.(1942). *Mere Christianity*. New York: HarperCollins.

Mayo Clinic (2015). *High blood pressure and sex: Overcome the challenges*. [Online] Available from: http://www.mayoclinic.org/diseases-conditions/high-blood-pressure/in-depth/high-blood-pressure-and-sex/art-20044209. [Accessed 19th January, 2016].

Moyo, D. (2009). *Dead Aid: Why Aid is not working and how there is another way for Africa*. London: Penguin Books.

Munroe, M. (2002). *The Purpose and Power of Love and Marriage*. Shippensburg, PA: Destiny Image.

National Institute of Diabetes and Digestive and
    Kidney Diseases (2016). *Causes of
    Diabetes*.[Online] Available from:
    http://www.niddk.nih.gov/health-
    information/health-topics/Diabetes/causes-
    diabetes/Pages/index.aspx. [Accessed: 19th
    January, 2016].

WebMD(2016). *Erectile Dysfunction Health
    Center*. [Online] Available from:
    http://www.webmd.com/erectile-
    dysfunction/guide/ed-diabetes. [Accessed 20th
    January, 2016].

World Bank (2016). *Population Data.* [Online]
    Available from:
    http://data.worldbank.org/indicator/SP.POP.T
    OTL. [Accessed 5th March, 2016].

Index

G

gameo, xxiii
glucose, 183, 184

H

Holes in the wall, 72
hunter-gatherer age, 103
hypertension, 89, 95, 185

I

*IMPROVE YOUR
FINANCIAL IQ*, 131
inappropriate relationship,
155, 156, 170
industrial age, 104
information age, 104
insanity, 88
insulin, 183, 184

K

Kiyosaki, Robert, 108

L

Lee, Kuan Yew, 193, 197
Lewis, C.S., 59, 64, 197
listening, 33, 48, 49, 72, 157
love, 65, 120, 197
lust, 40, 146, 155, 171

M

maturity, 53, 69, 96

menstruation, 189
mentee, 119
mentor, xxv, 82, 108, 119,
133, 134
mentorship, 114, 119, 132
misunderstandings, 52, 67
money, xii, 47, 76, 77, 80,
91, 94, 97, 100, 106, 108,
124, 125, 126, 127, 128,
130, 163, 164, 170, 177,
178
moral support to wife, 178
multiply thy conception,
189
Munroe, Myles, xxiii, xxiv,
47, 48, 77, 197

N

Norah, Phiri, xxiv, 47, 48,
125, 164, 165

O

orgasm, 40, 41, 42
Original Sin, 189, 190

P

Philippines, 191
planning, 49, 94, 98, 100,
105, 106, 121, 126, 159,
186, 187, 190, 191
political-correctness in
marriage, 172
prayer therapy, 52
pregnancy, 191

Notes

Notes

Notes

Notes

Notes

Notes

Notes

Notes

Notes

Notes

Notes

Notes

Notes

www.ingramcontent.com/pod-product-compliance
Lightning Source LLC
Chambersburg PA
CBHW021950120726
47992CB00001B/233